MW01630012

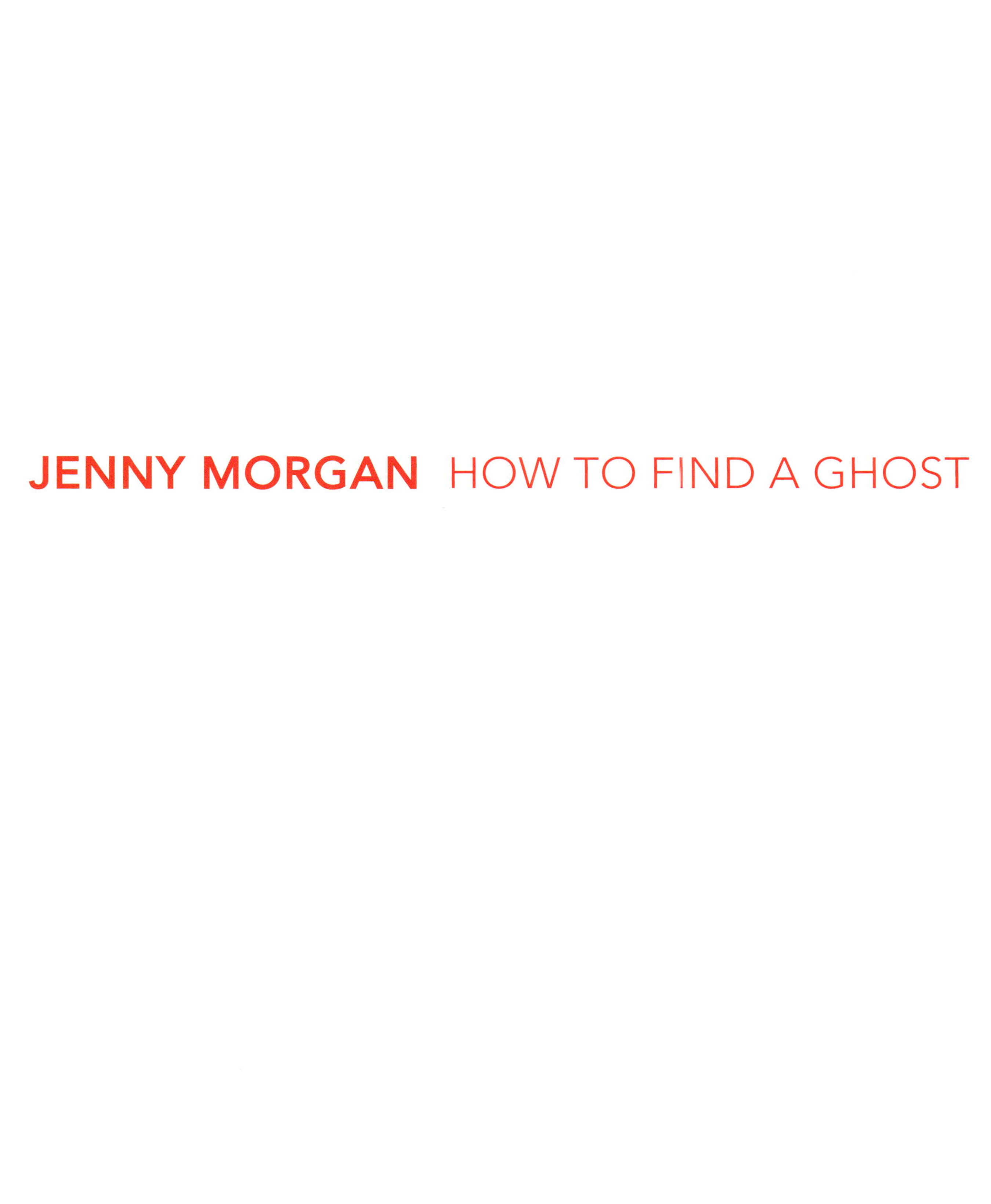

JENNY MORGAN HOW TO FIND A GHOST

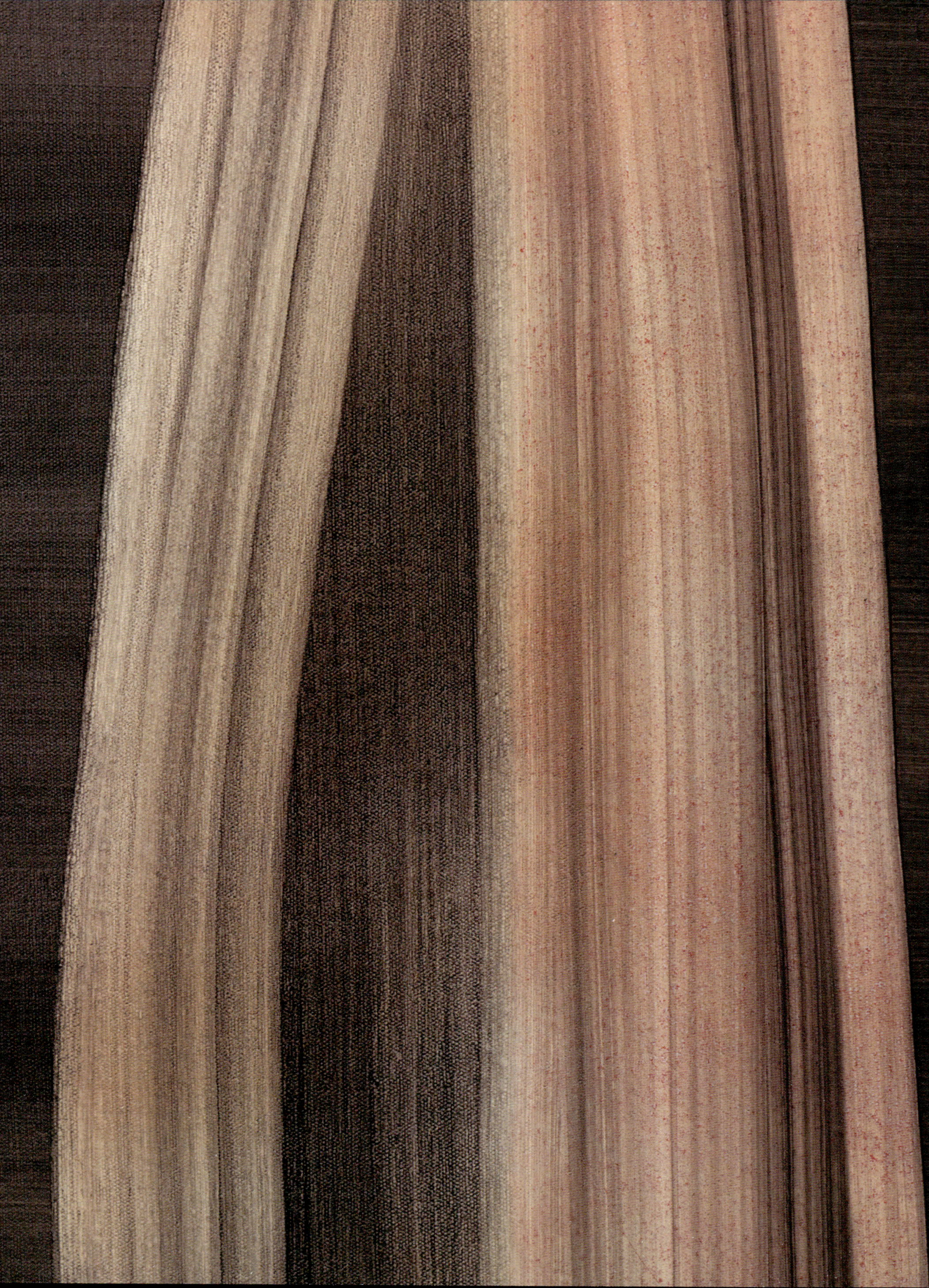

JENNY MORGAN HOW TO FIND A GHOST

BENJAMIN GENOCCHIO

INTRODUCTION
TESS SOL SCHWAB

DRISCOLL | BABCOCK

ISBN: 978-0-9898062-1-3

Design: Driscoll Babcock Galleries
Printing: Cosmos Communications
Photography: All photography © 2013 Max Yawney, except:
© 2013 Jessie Adler: pp. 5, 15, 54-55, 62

Library of Congress Cataloguing-in-Publication Data is available
        Genocchio, Benjamin
        Jenny Morgan: How To Find A Ghost
        with Introduction by Tess Sol Schwab
        1st Edition
        Includes biographical references

Jenny Morgan is exclusively represented by Driscoll Babcock Galleries
525 West 25th Street
New York, NY 10001
+1 212.767.1852
info@driscollbabcock.com   www.driscollbabcock.com

This catalogue is published to accompany the exhibition
Jenny Morgan: How To Find A Ghost
Driscoll Babcock Galleries
October 17 – November 23, 2013

Front cover: SHIFT, 2013, p. 23 (detail)
Back cover: GREAT DIVIDE, 2013, p. 17 (detail)
Frontispiece: GREAT DIVIDE, 2013, p. 17 (detail)

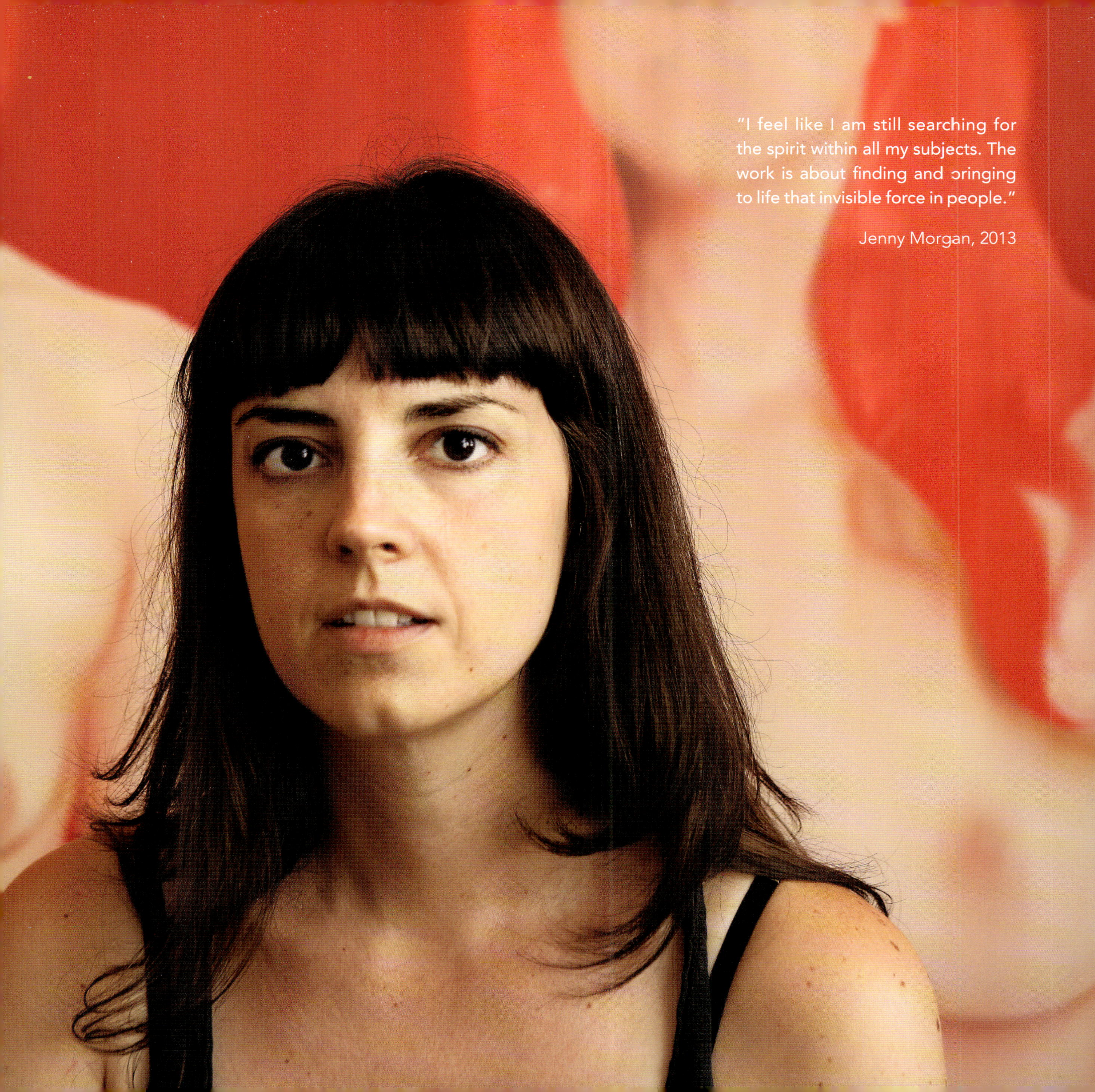

"I feel like I am still searching for the spirit within all my subjects. The work is about finding and bringing to life that invisible force in people."

Jenny Morgan, 2013

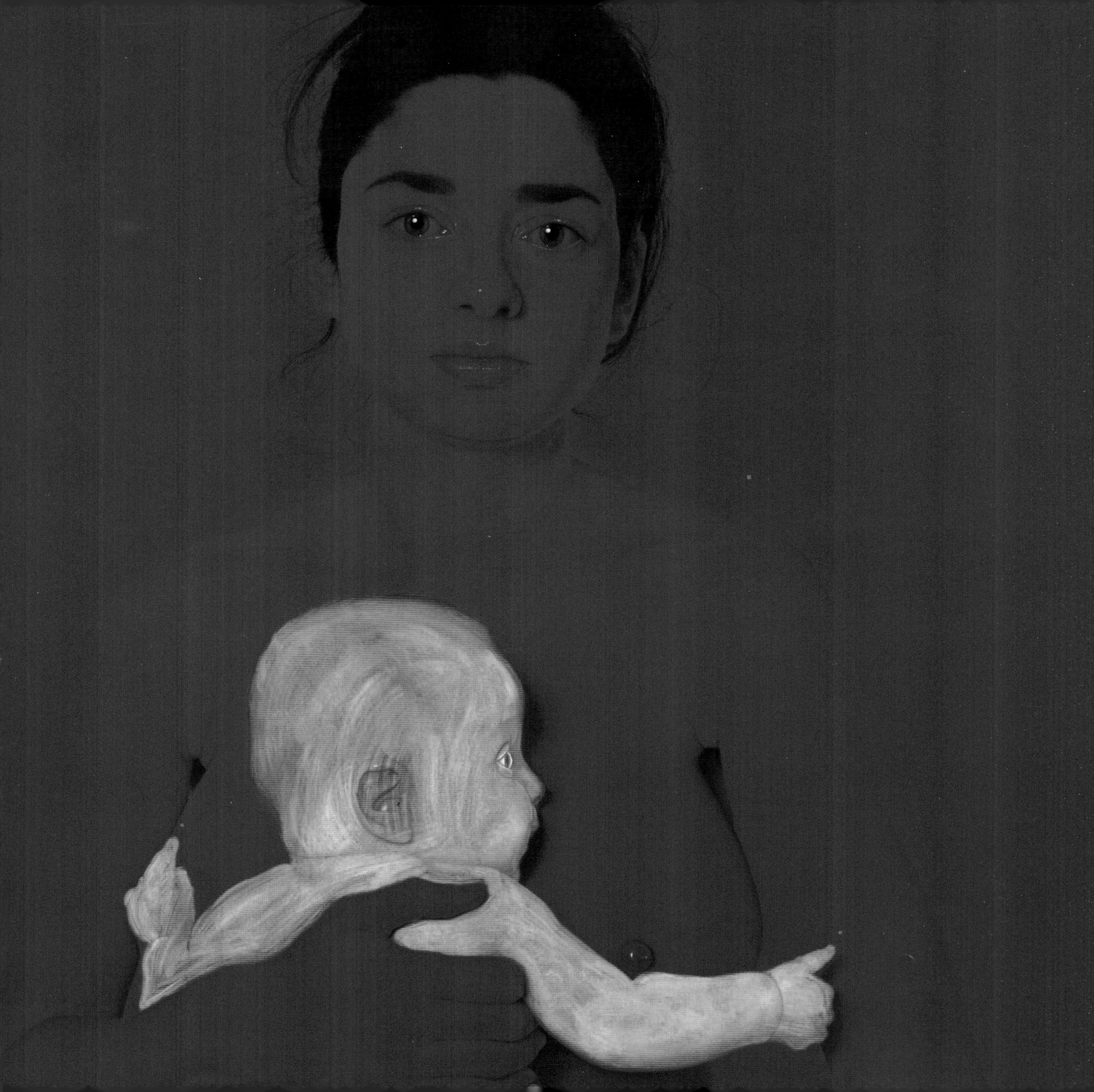

APPREHENDING THE APPARITION
Tess Sol Schwab

Jenny Morgan is looking for something. Meeting her, one is immediately struck by her alert and beautifully formed eyes—windows to her inner being and the primary tools in her search for the spirit, the soul, the essence of others. She has been looking since she was a young girl, when she would spend her playtime hunting for ghosts. An unusually curious and intellectually quick child, she carried with her an intuitive feeling and innate knowledge that there was more to a person than just his or her physical body, more to a home than the space it occupied and contained.

However, as she grew into a visual person, Morgan progressively understood this feeling that knowledge was not enough—seeing was truly believing. How then could she express these sensations that were so real to her, but which had no perceptual, tangible or physical embodiment, and which she lacked a language to describe? At age 8, Morgan found a key to this world she knew existed, but had no way of accessing—a literal "how-to" book entitled *How to Find a Ghost* by James M. Deem, published in 1988 by Houghton Mifflin. Still considered by Morgan to be one of the most influential books of her life, *How to Find a Ghost* provided step-by-step instructions to discover the spirits around her. It both validated her feelings and provided a crucial outlet for her budding exploration of spirituality. It introduced the possibility that she could describe and record the phenomena she experienced.

While no longer hunting for literal ghosts, this constant search for something felt and known, but unseen—and the struggle to express that—remains. Morgan's paintings break through the ideals of traditionalist realism and capture her striking intensity and psychological experience. Focusing on people she is close to—friends, family and her own visage—she brings forward the connection she has with her sitters, giving her subjects not only a physical presence, but embodying their spiritual beings. This is knowledge and feeling of a high order.

Left: Detail of MOTHER, 2013, page 33

Such is the case in MOTHER, 2013, which presents the artist's close friend and her friend's six month-old baby. Not just a simple portrait, the work is a testament to the deep and undeniable connection between mother and child. Held close, the child is physically one with her mother, and the love and joy they share is evident. A closer look reveals small turquoise dots emanating from the baby's fingertips. Often Morgan employs these dots, circles, orbs in her paintings as a symbol for the spirit or soul. Here the child's spirit is intricately tied to her mother, as the cool blue of those iconic dots rest against the primal red of the mother's body. Yet even with the overwhelming positivity within the work, there is a flicker of unease—a heaviness in the eyes, a rawness to the skin. It would be impossible to ignore this other layer. What the artist had originally thought of as a "sweet homage" evolved into a depiction of personal uncertainty. Morgan's portrayal of this mother and child became a self-portrait of her own deep fears about her path to motherhood.

Further self-reflection is evident in SHIFT, 2013. In this work Morgan depicts herself with wisps of hair radiating outward, as if charged with an electric current. Part of her face has been blurred by a sweeping brushstroke, but one eye glows with a yellow frequency, a lighthouse's Fresnel lens breaking through the fog. A large red dot—a metaphorical third-eye—is placed on the top of her head. The third-eye is thought to provide perception beyond visible sight and process the energy that surrounds us, and Morgan creates hers not by placing a dot upon her head, but by going further into the canvas and revealing the work's red under-painting. This focus on eyes and sight symbolizes a desire to see and know the unknowable—a universal desire when faced with an uncertain future—and an apt metaphor during a period when the artist's life was in transition and "shifting" from one chapter of her life to another.

With each change and new discovery in her life, one things remains constant: Morgan's devotion to her arcing quest—the quest to find the ghost, the spirit, the apparition—and make it appear.

Right: Detail of SHIFT, 2013, page 23

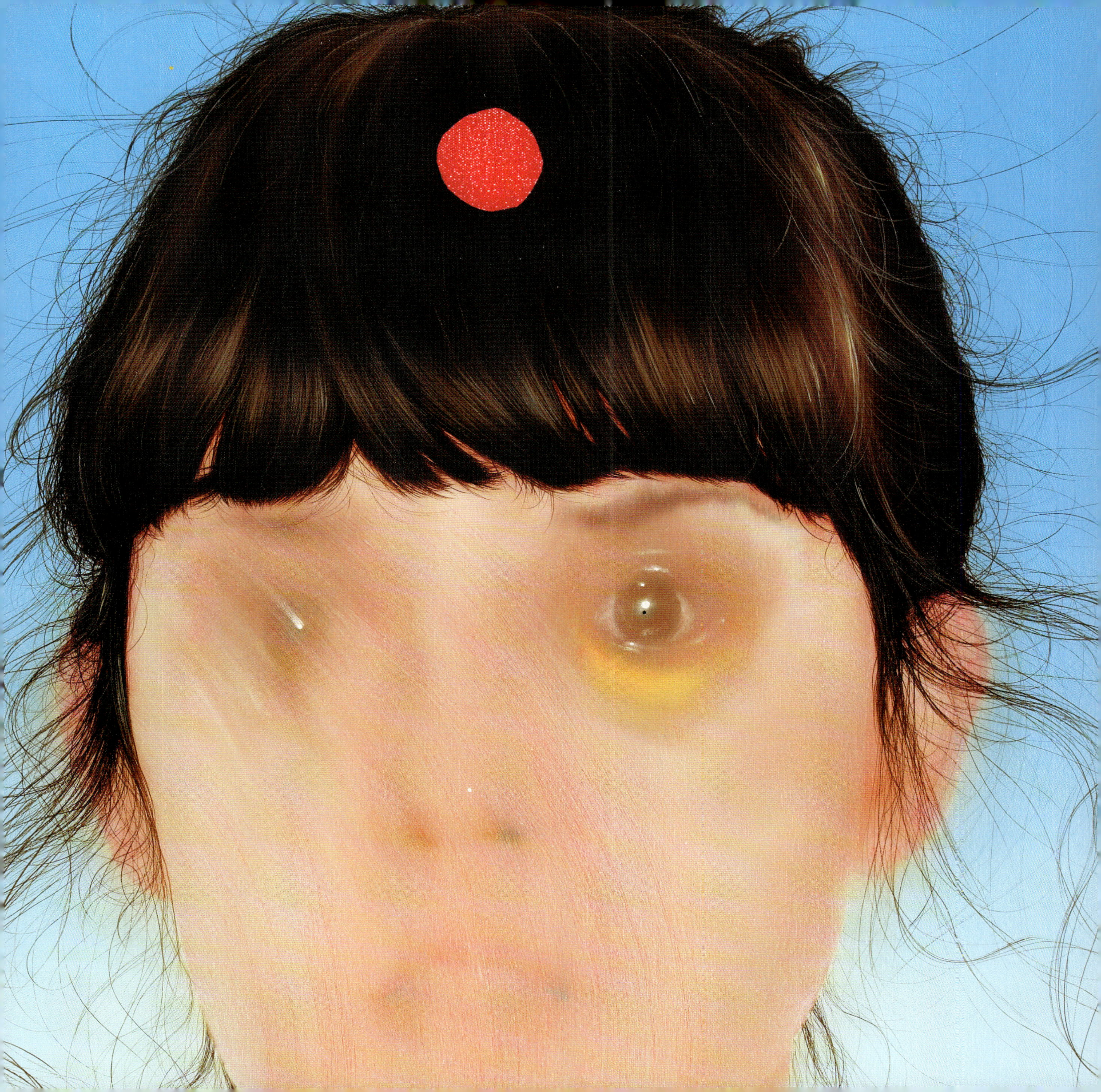

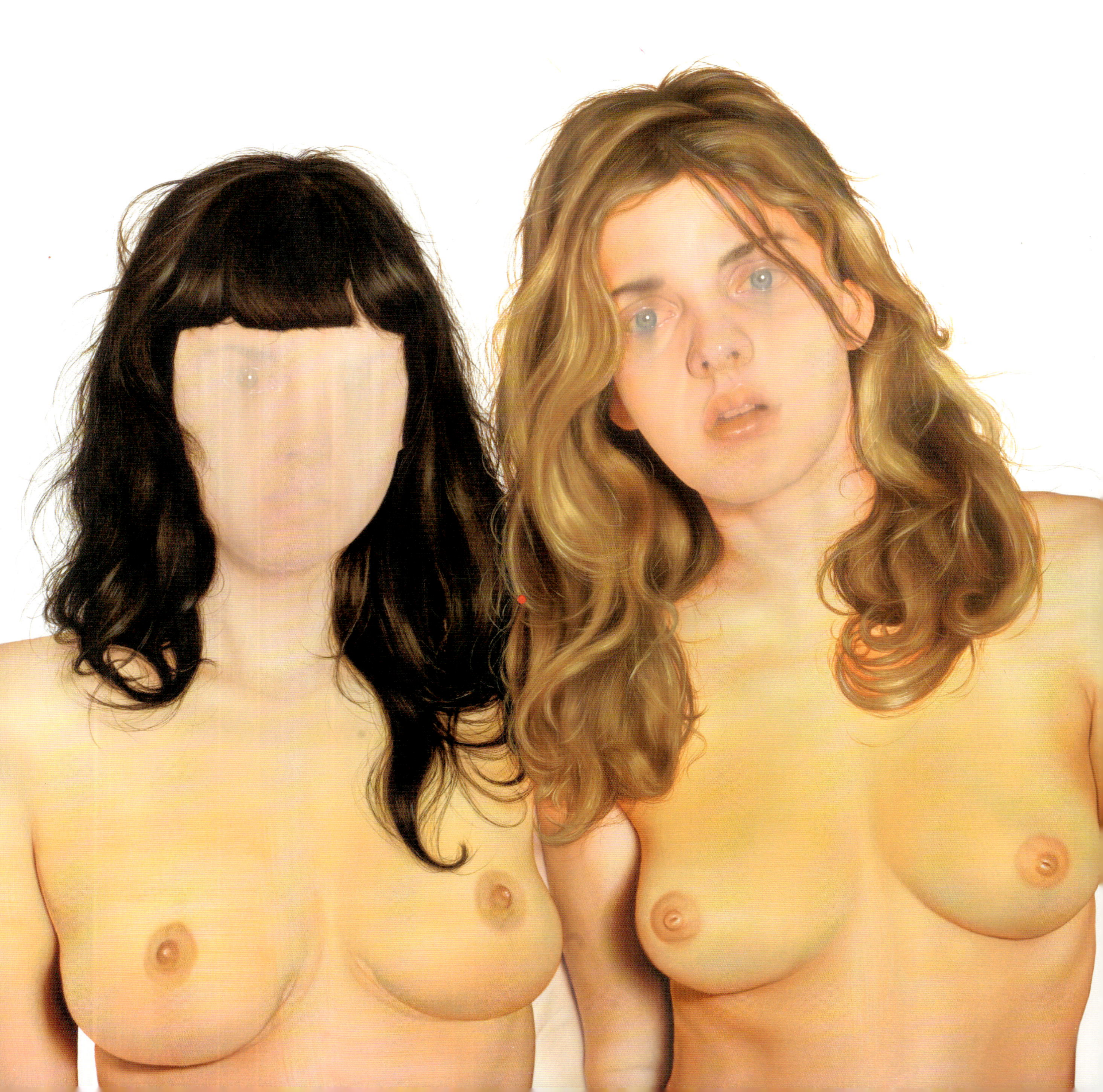

JENNY MORGAN'S NAKED TRUTH

Benjamin Genocchio

What can we know for certain? The French philosopher René Descartes staked his peg in the hard ground of reason, arguing that there was little of which we could be certain beyond the proposition that to think is to exist. He was right in a way; being conscious of our own existence is the first step towards understanding. But he was also wrong: to exist is to feel, and feelings can be more accurate than thoughts.

Feelings can also be more dangerous, more powerful because they aren't subject to reason. They remain hidden, bubbling, sometimes bursting forth suddenly without consciousness or control. Artists know this, because they frequently work this way, and by their nature tend to be exceptionally sensitive to feelings. This is one of the reasons art has long been associated with ideas of truth.

I feel therefore I am: that's the proposition Jenny Morgan puts forth in her pictures. Like Descartes, she doubts everything, but rebuilds her faith in herself, in others and in the world on the foundation of feelings. She trusts her instincts to guide her creative decisions in the studio. To her credit, the act of painting can sometimes bring her to tears.

Her faith in feelings encompasses both the form and the content of the pictures. She works with a small number of subjects, people she knows, whom she trusts and who in turn trust her. It is not complicated: she goes to their home, with a camera and asks them to take off their clothes. Sitting in her small, self-contained studio in Bushwick the artist told me that in the past, she had painted fabric, and it just felt flat and cold and unreal. From that point onward she felt like clothes were a distraction, a barrier to truth. She is probably right about this: looking at her paintings, the naked figures are both painfully exposed and vulnerable, but simultaneously human and real.

The photographic images are then a basis for portraits, which always somehow verge on self-portraits. Through painting others, she reveals herself. Perhaps this is why she only

Left: Detail of YOU TO ME, 2013, page 25

paints people she knows and trusts. She has to be close emotionally to her subjects, as people, in order to capture their inner spirit, energy and aura, which is the real subject of her art. If she does not have feelings for her subjects she cannot paint them, she says, which makes sense. "It feels forced and untrue," she told me, "and there is no depth." Painting for her is about a connection, emotional as much as psychological. She delves deep into human emotions, digs under the skin of her subjects, to get to know and show them better.

Painting for her is also, increasingly, about abstraction. This new series of pictures represents an important, even significant departure for the 31-year old Salt Lake City, Utah-born and raised, but now Brooklyn-based artist. Seven years of focused painting of the human figure is gradually giving way to a more experimental, even playful style in which faces dissolve, hair frays and bodies bleed.

Classically trained as a painter of figures, Morgan has mastered the exacting discipline of correctly depicting the human anatomy—look at the hands and feet of her figures and you will see an artist at ease with the most difficult elements of a subject matter. She can paint the human body with love, grace and skill. But her skills were stifling her progress—letting go of perfection, she realized, opened the door to creativity.

Many figurative painters have trodden this path. Picasso, for example, found a voice of his own on the road to abstraction from realism. Francis Bacon and Lucien Freud, as well as Jenny Saville, more recently, may also be mentioned here, to name artists whose work Morgan admires. Importantly, none of these artists ever renounced the figure as primary subject matter; they all found ways of making it seem more real, much like Morgan, by zeroing in on emotional and psychological connections.

Sometimes the abstraction is barely perceptible, like the disheveled and knotty ball of dark hair falling over the left shoulder of the female figure in WE ARE NOT ALONE, 2013. But this intentional imperfection in the painting is brilliantly apt and in turn profoundly real, for the weary sadness in her eyes and smile suggests someone for whom other, pressing worries cloud her mind. She isn't thinking about her hair.

The artist takes the process of abstraction quite a bit further in THE FLOOD, 2013, in which a relatively conventional portrait of a young woman with a mop of ginger-brown hair is rendered faceless using two violent gashes for eye sockets, a blurry frizz of hair, and a melted, blackened outline of a head and neck. She is rendered a mask, sapped of subjectivity in a way that feels like a violation. She appears lost, in a state of psychological pain or confusion. Perhaps she is still figuring out her life path.

Morgan's paintings are not unkind or cruel, for the figures are always shown with sensitivity and compassion. Furthermore, she is not shy at all of turning her direct, drilling gaze on herself, as in YOU TO ME, 2013, a large, powerful work in which the artist pairs a naked faceless self-portrait with that of a beautiful friend, Syrie, who exudes a confident sexuality. Morgan admires, longs for such sexual confidence, which is the real subject of this painting and a good illustration of the way in which her pictures are more about emotional and psychological states than about bodies.

Syrie appears in another picture, SYRIE AND THE CAT, 2013, naked and holding a cat. She is alluring and sexual, caressing the fluffy, sensual mass of the animal. This is as close as Morgan gets to sex in her paintings, associating her extremely beautiful and nubile friend with the witchy wiles and sensuality of a black cat. This painting is all about pussy, basically, the raw power of desire and its hold on the imagination.

Sometimes when the artist's motivations are more transparent it is tempting to read these paintings as life stories. That would be a mistake. They have no social, political or wider ideological or moral purpose. They are intensely private, psychological and closed off from the world, almost illustrational in their matter-of-factness. These are the inhabitants of "Jenny's World," projections of fact, and fantasy, to some degree.

Painting with this kind of intensity and focus is demanding, physically and mentally. No surprise to learn that the artist will complete as little as 15 small to medium-sized pictures a year, each taking two to three weeks to finish up. Larger ones can take her up to a month to complete. She works on multiple paintings at the same time so she can bounce about between them. This is slow art, with careful looking required.

Taking time to look at Morgan's paintings reveals many subtle, wonderful details: in MENTOR, 2012, the naked figure's legs have turned a red-orange, suggesting that she is on fire and about to go up in smoke. Or the red dots that have started to appear in several new paintings, made using tiny circles of tape around which the artist paints, revealing the original red acrylic base underneath.

It is good to see the artist relaxing a little, having fun with her pictures. It is a brave, but positive progression and one that points to important, possibly brilliant things to come. Morgan is still looking for truth, like the Greek philosopher Diogenes of Sinope who is said to have wandered the marketplace in Athens in daylight with a burning oil lamp, in search, he said, "of an honest man." With her own new, improved torch, Morgan remains in touch with human emotions, but navigates the depths of the soul to let us view more clearly—for better and for worse—what it means to be human.

Right: Jenny Morgan in her studio, Brooklyn, New York, 2013

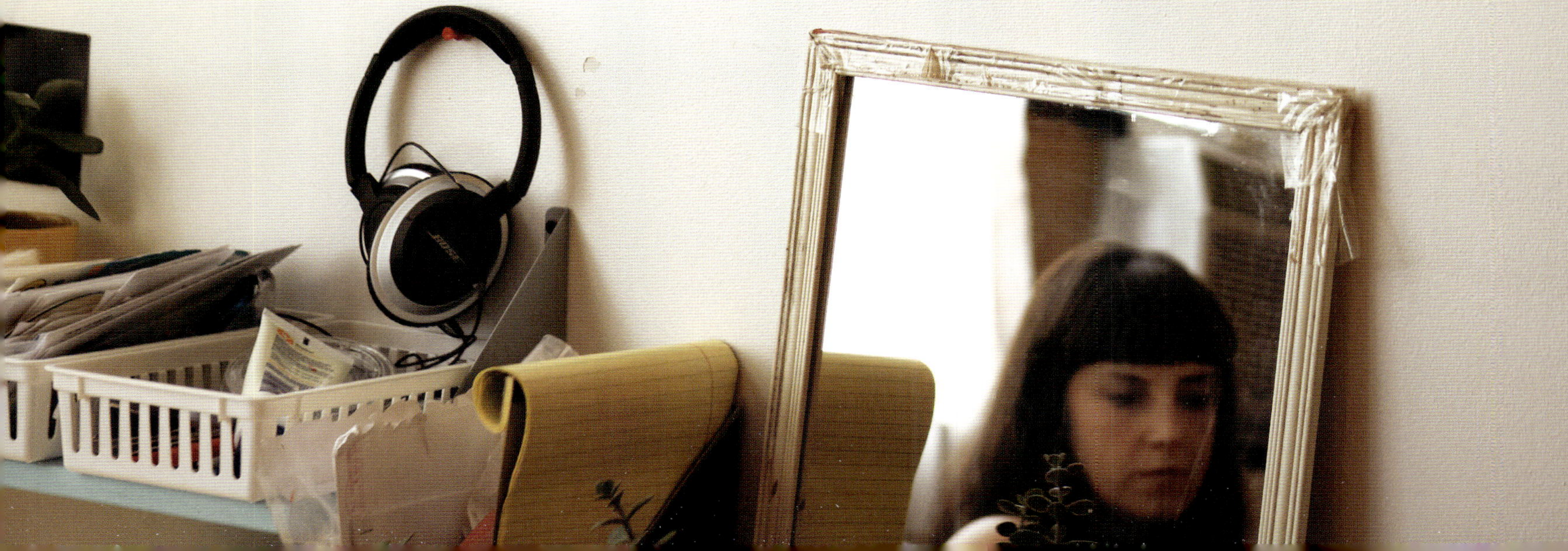

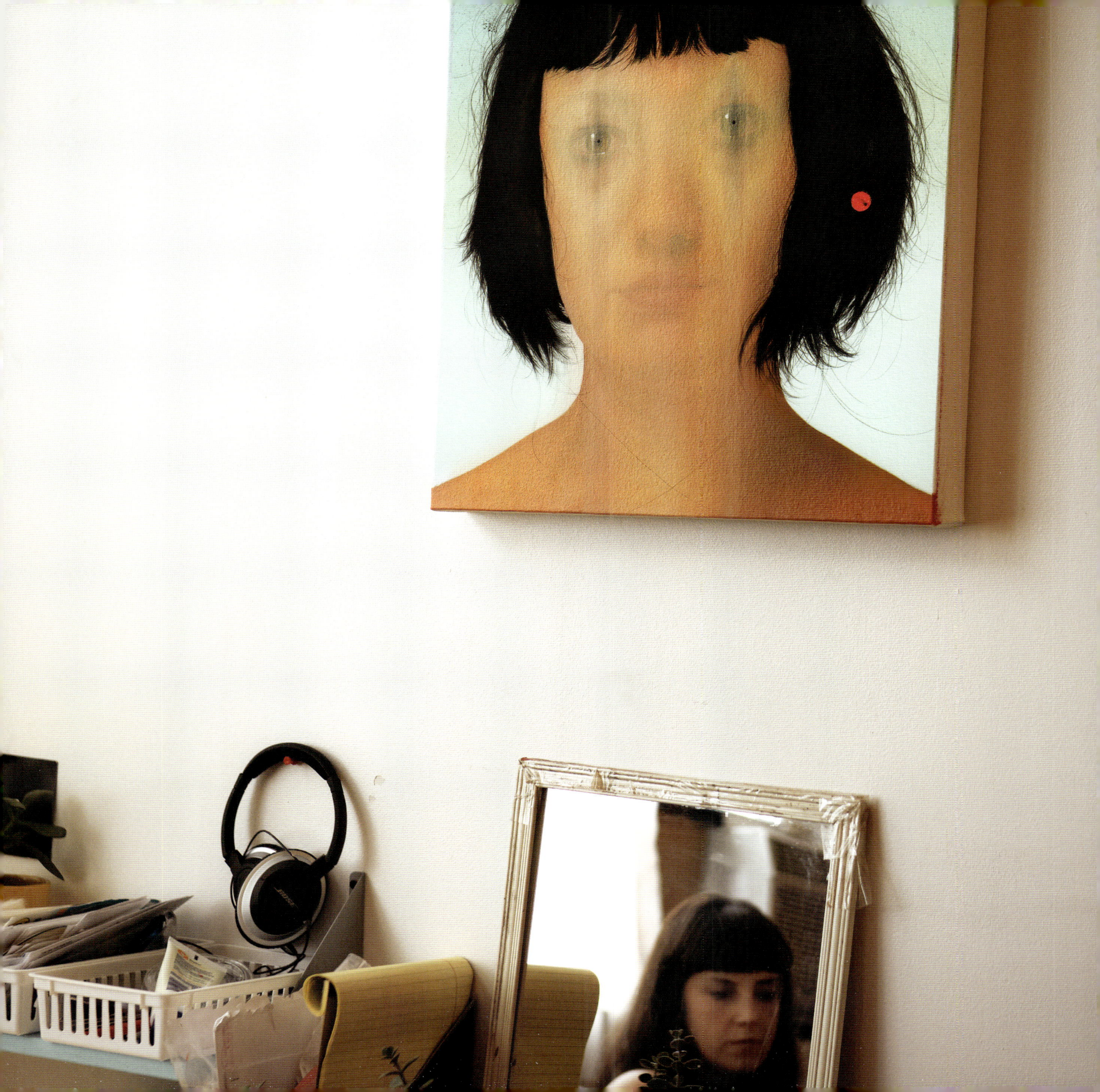

GREAT DIVIDE   2013   Oil on canvas   58 x 42 inches

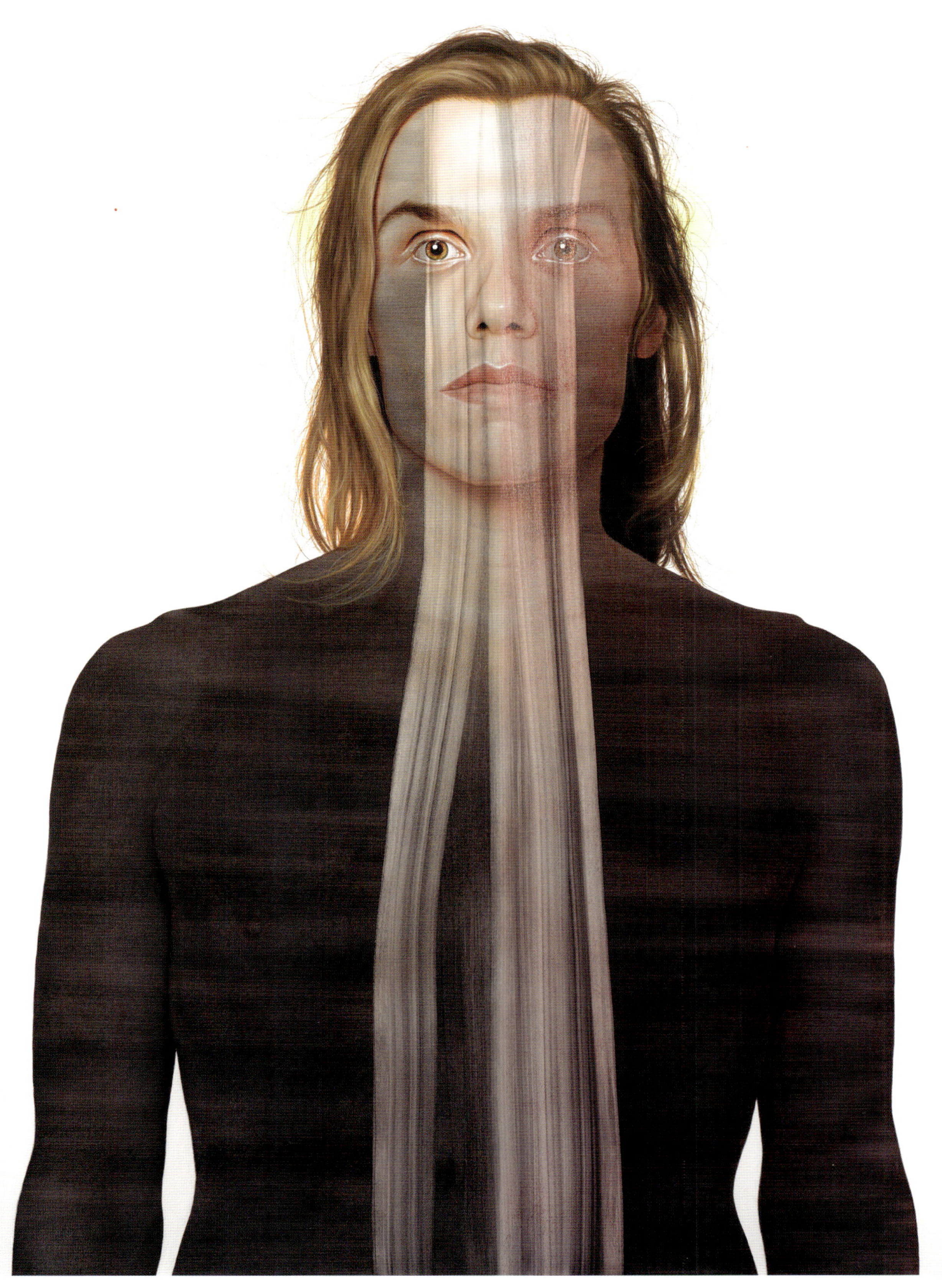

SYRIE AND THE CAT   2013   Oil on canvas   76 x 54 inches
Private Collection, New York

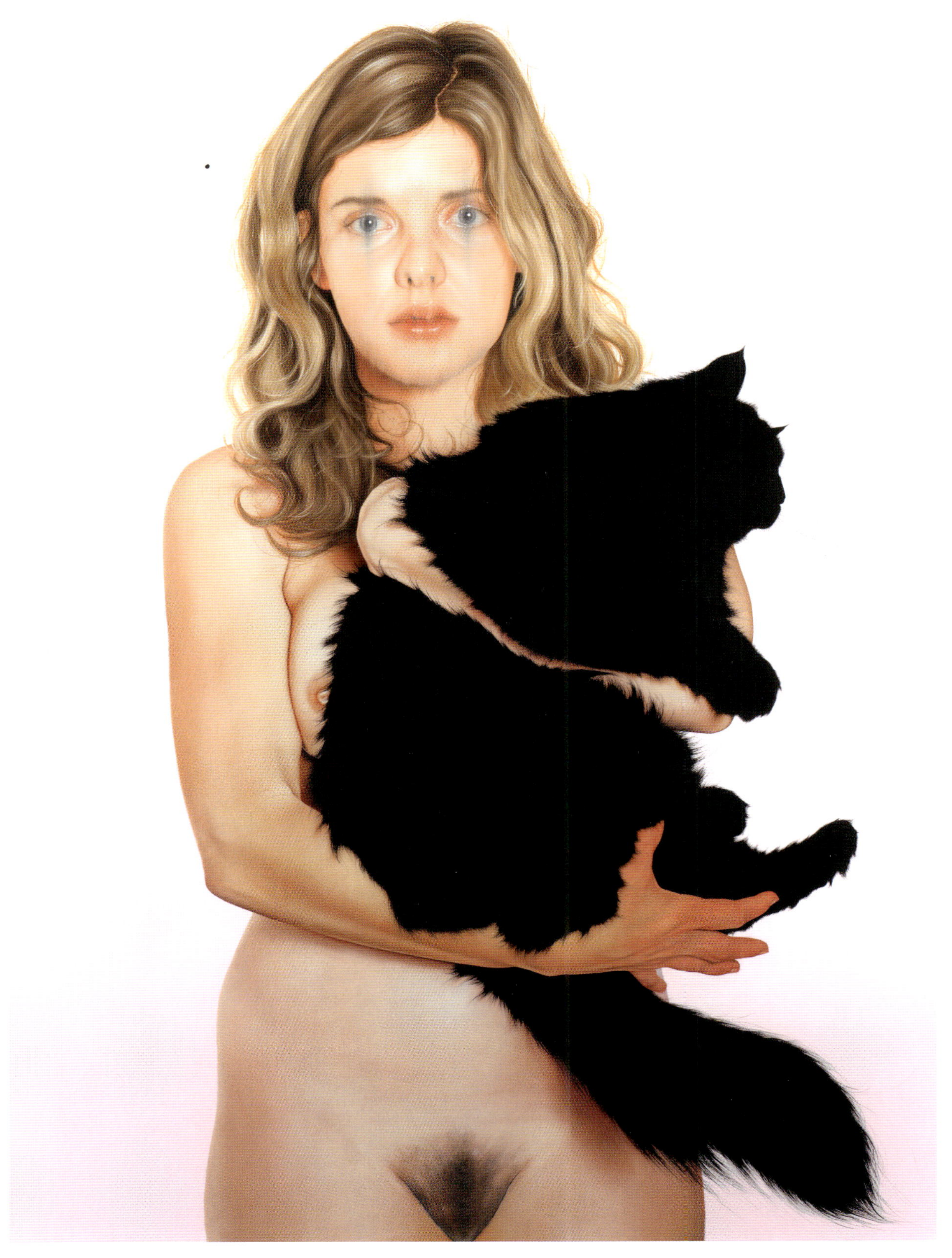

THE FLOOD   2013   Oil on canvas   36 x 30 inches

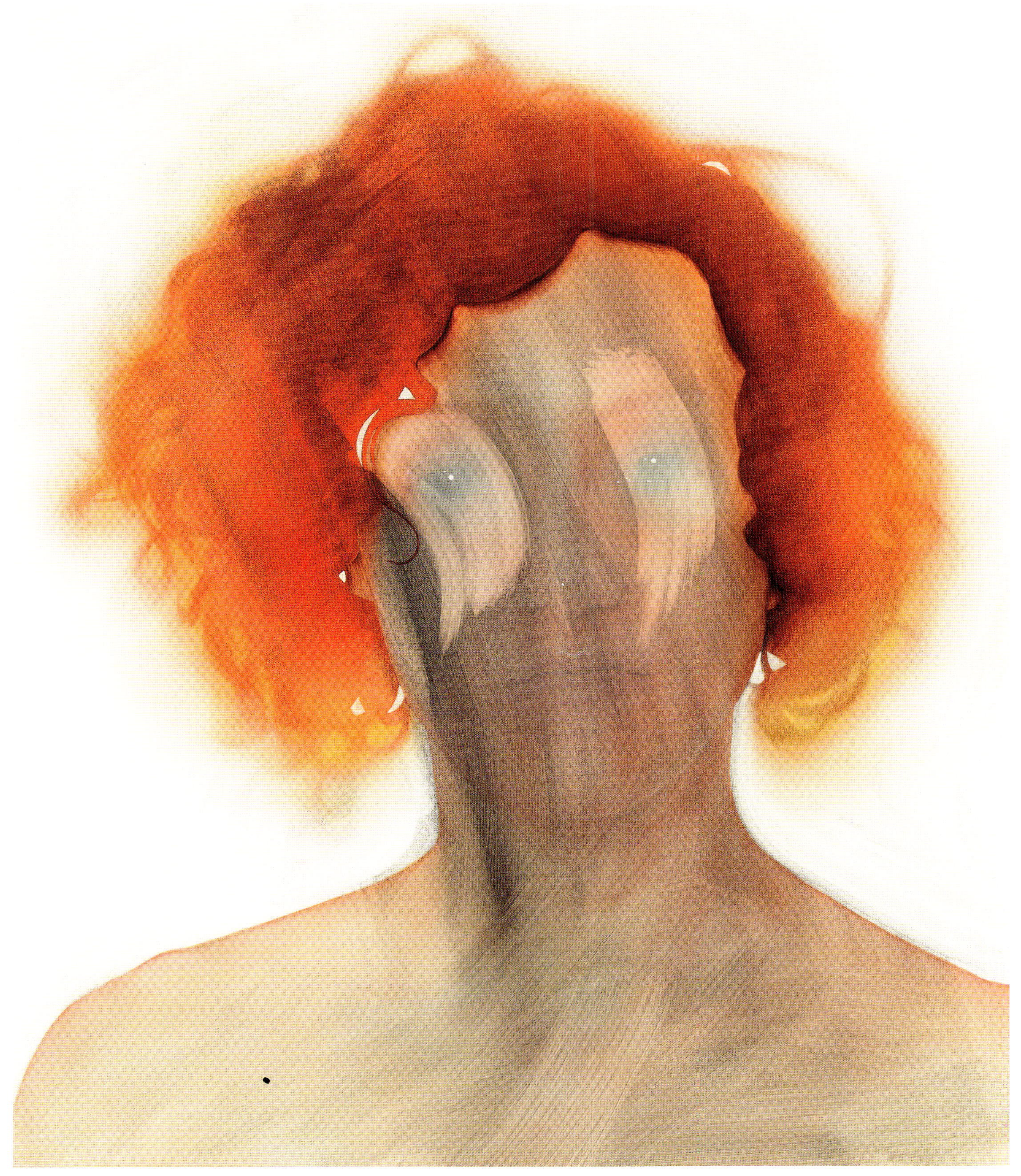

SHIFT   2013   Oil on canvas   38 x 32 inches

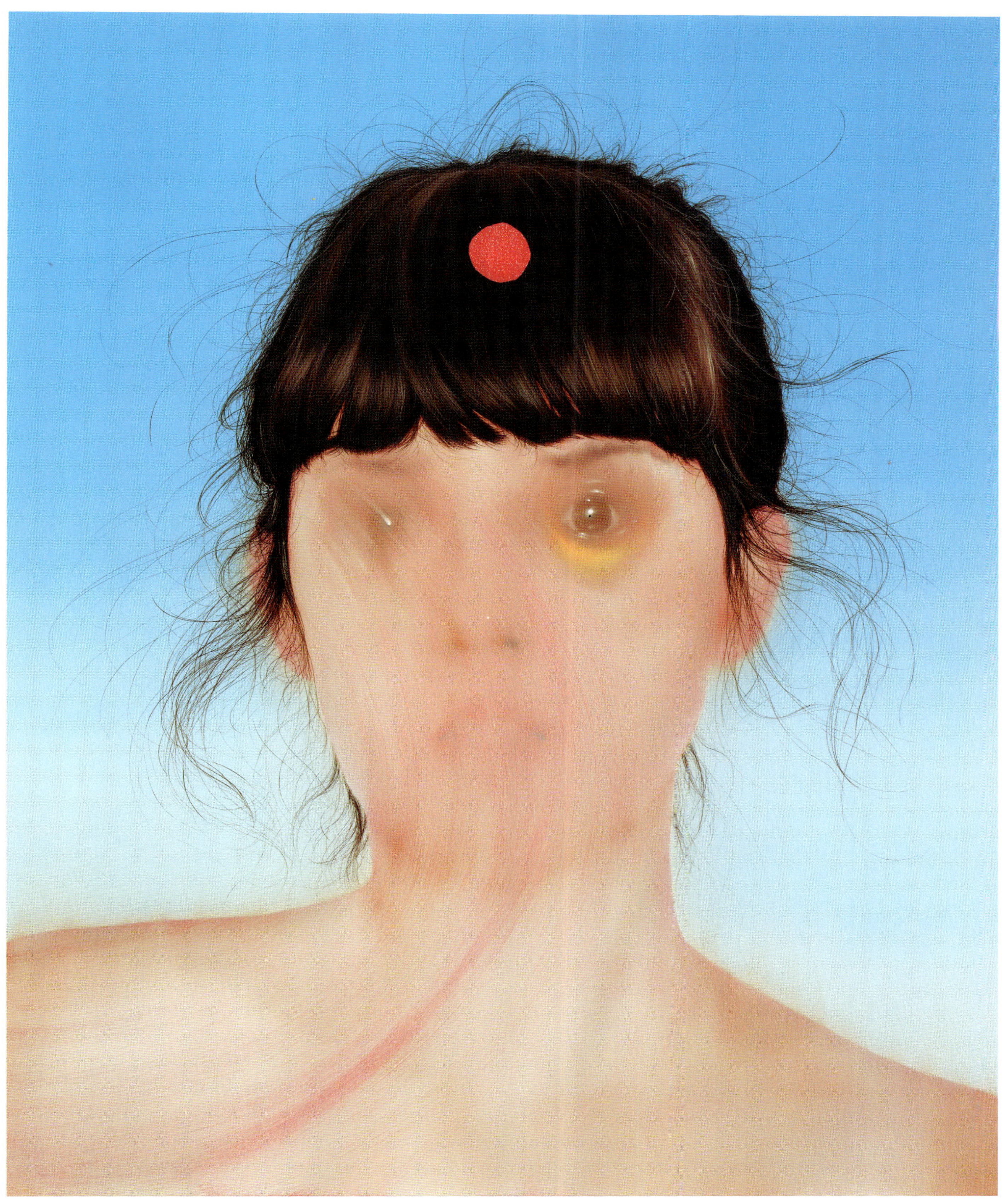

YOU TO ME   2013   Oil on canvas   92 x 78 inches
Private Collection, London

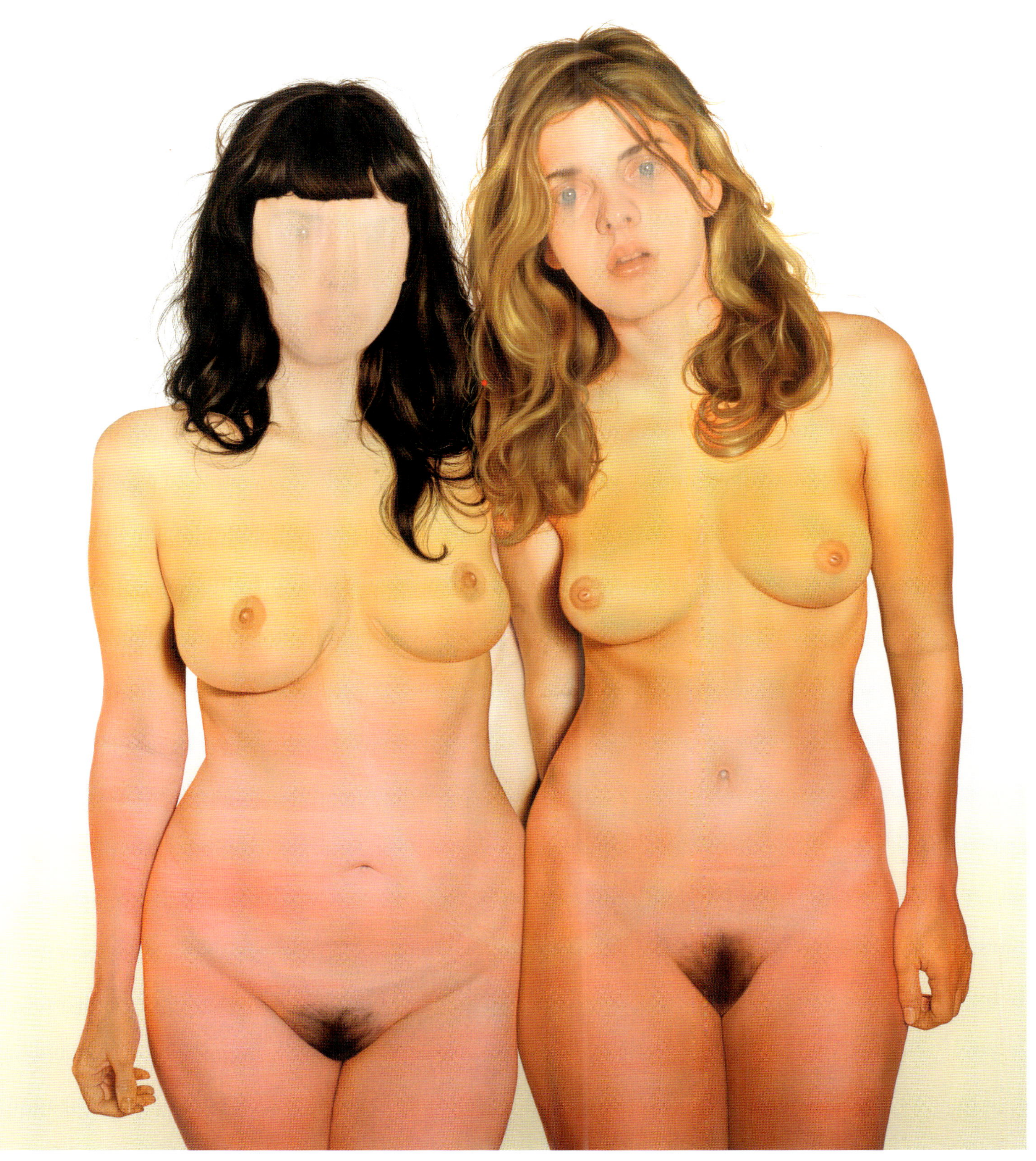

COSMIC GIGGLE   2013   Oil on canvas   24 x 20 ¾ inches

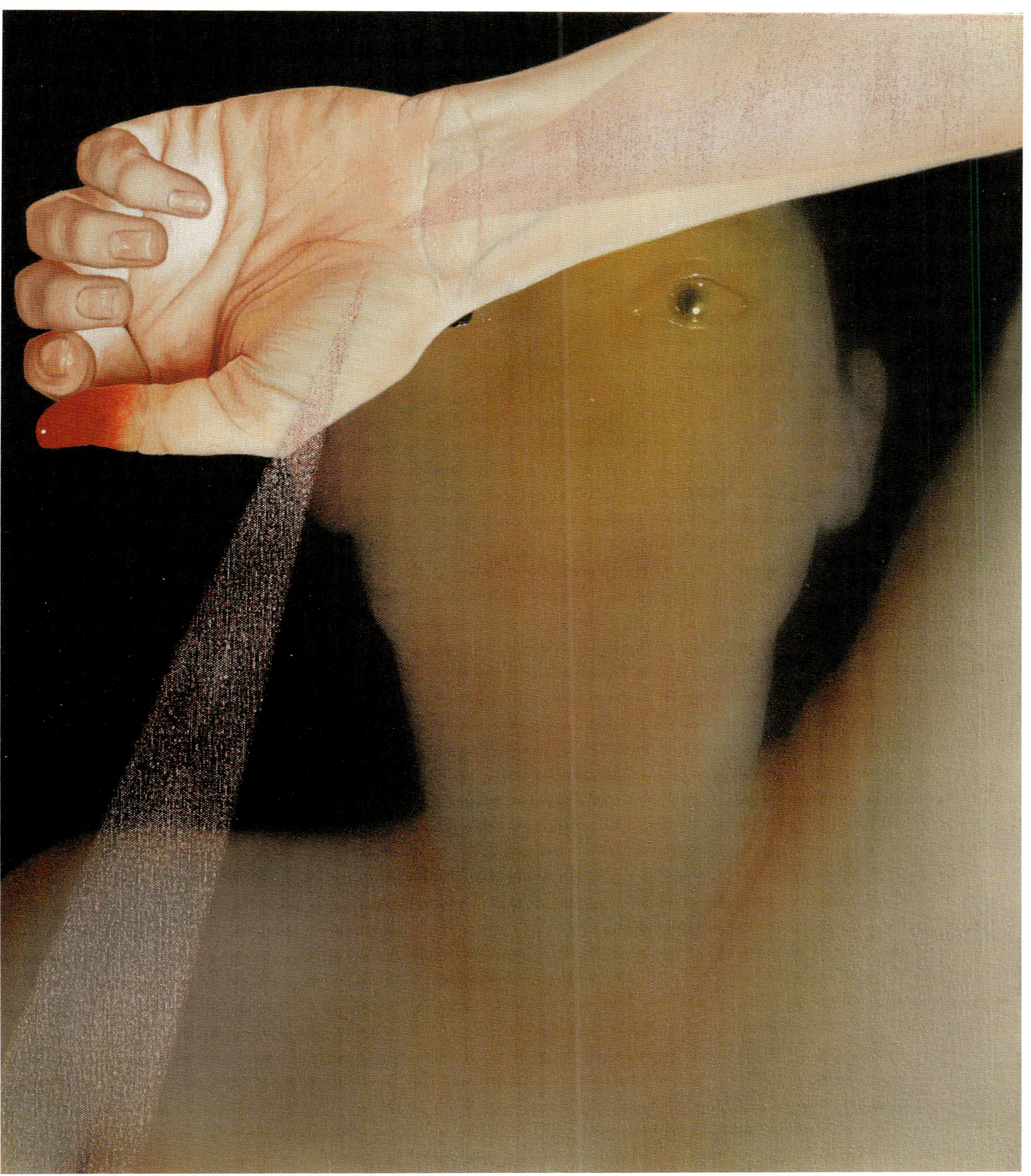

TRANSCENDENTAL SUPRA-MENTAL   2013   Oil on canvas   90 x 78 inches

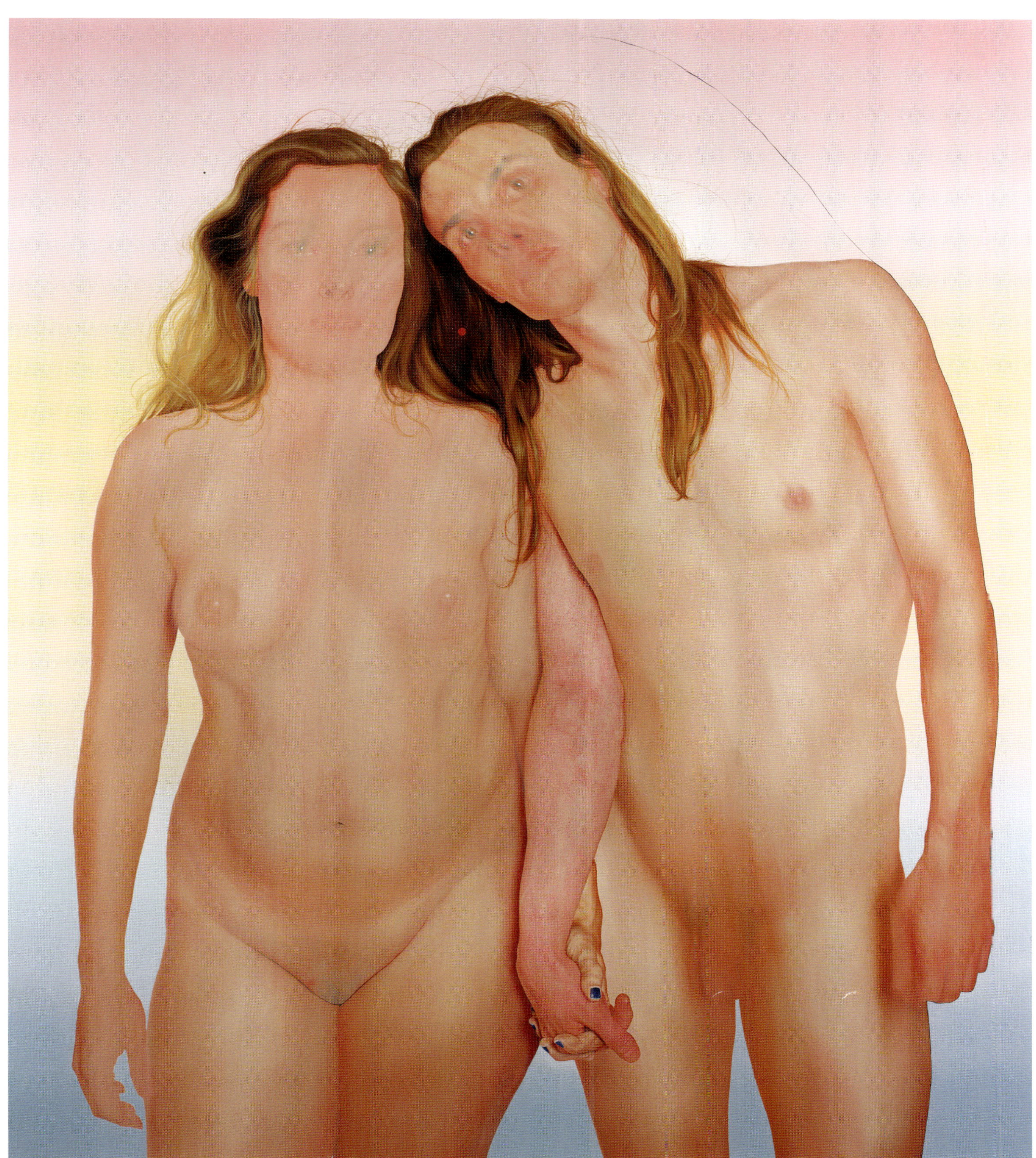

EXIT   2013   Oil on canvas   25 x 21 inches
Private Collection, New York

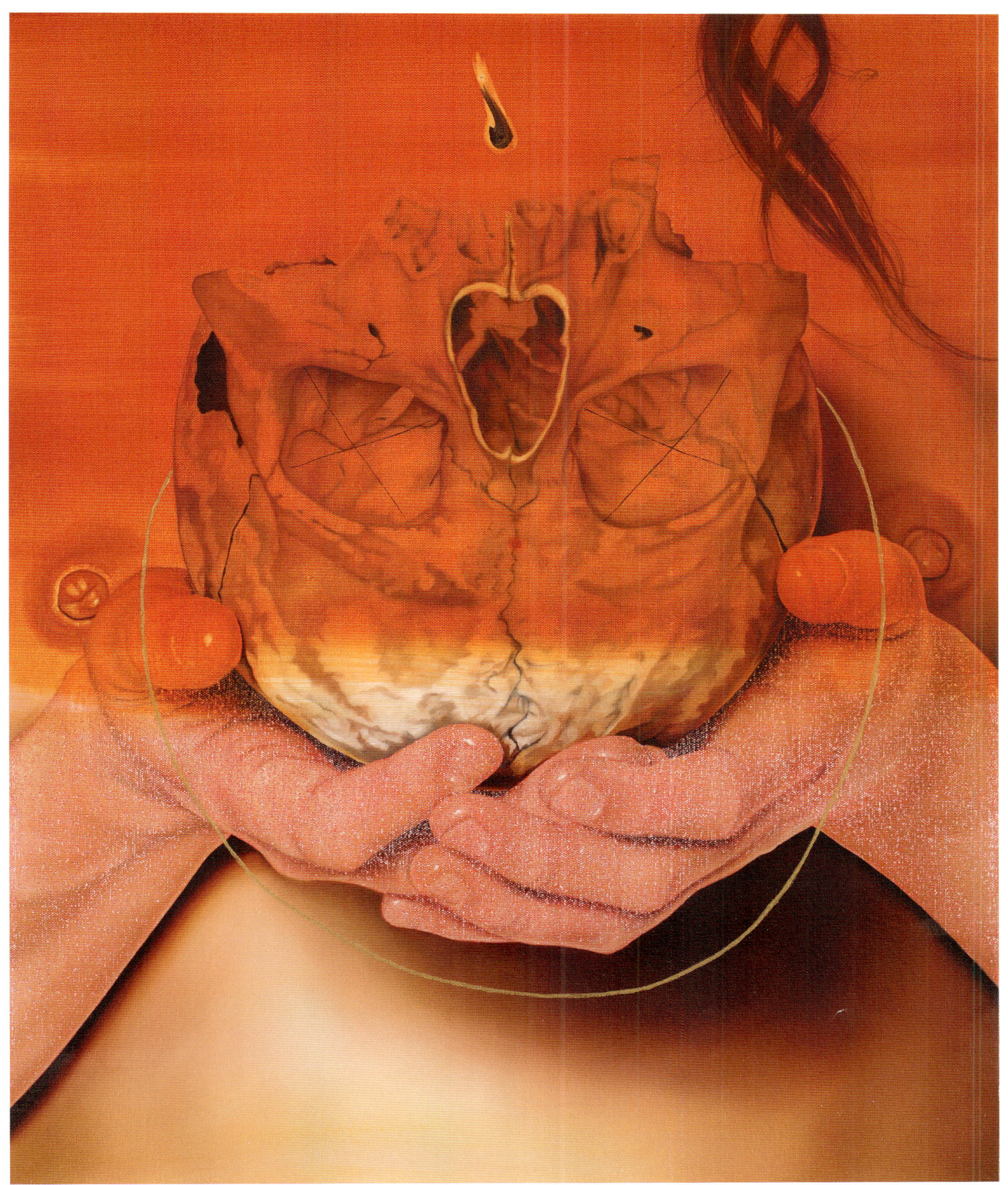

MOTHER   2013   Oil on canvas   90 x 56 inches

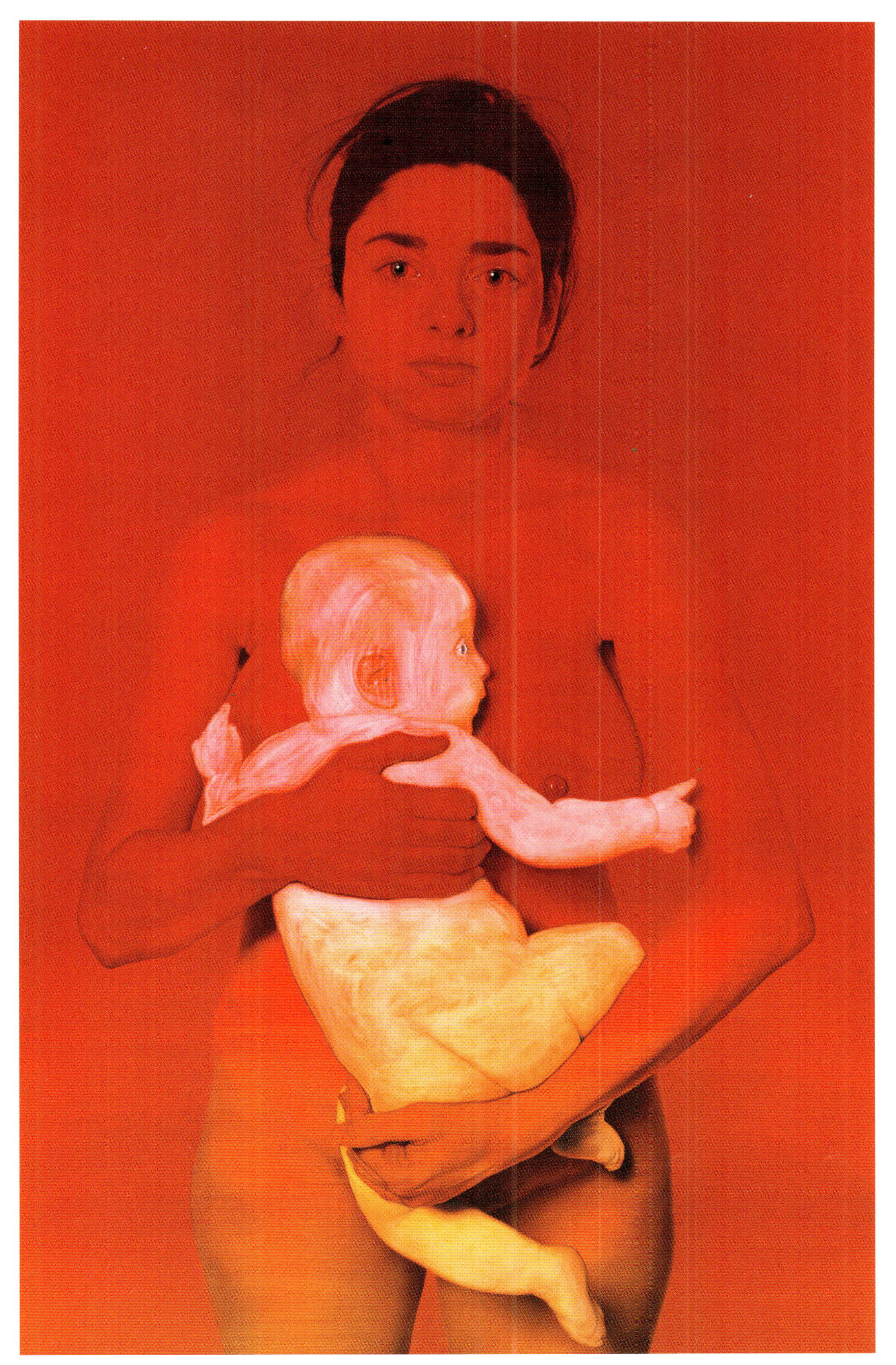

SEEING IS BELIEVING   2013   Oil on canvas   24 x 19 inches

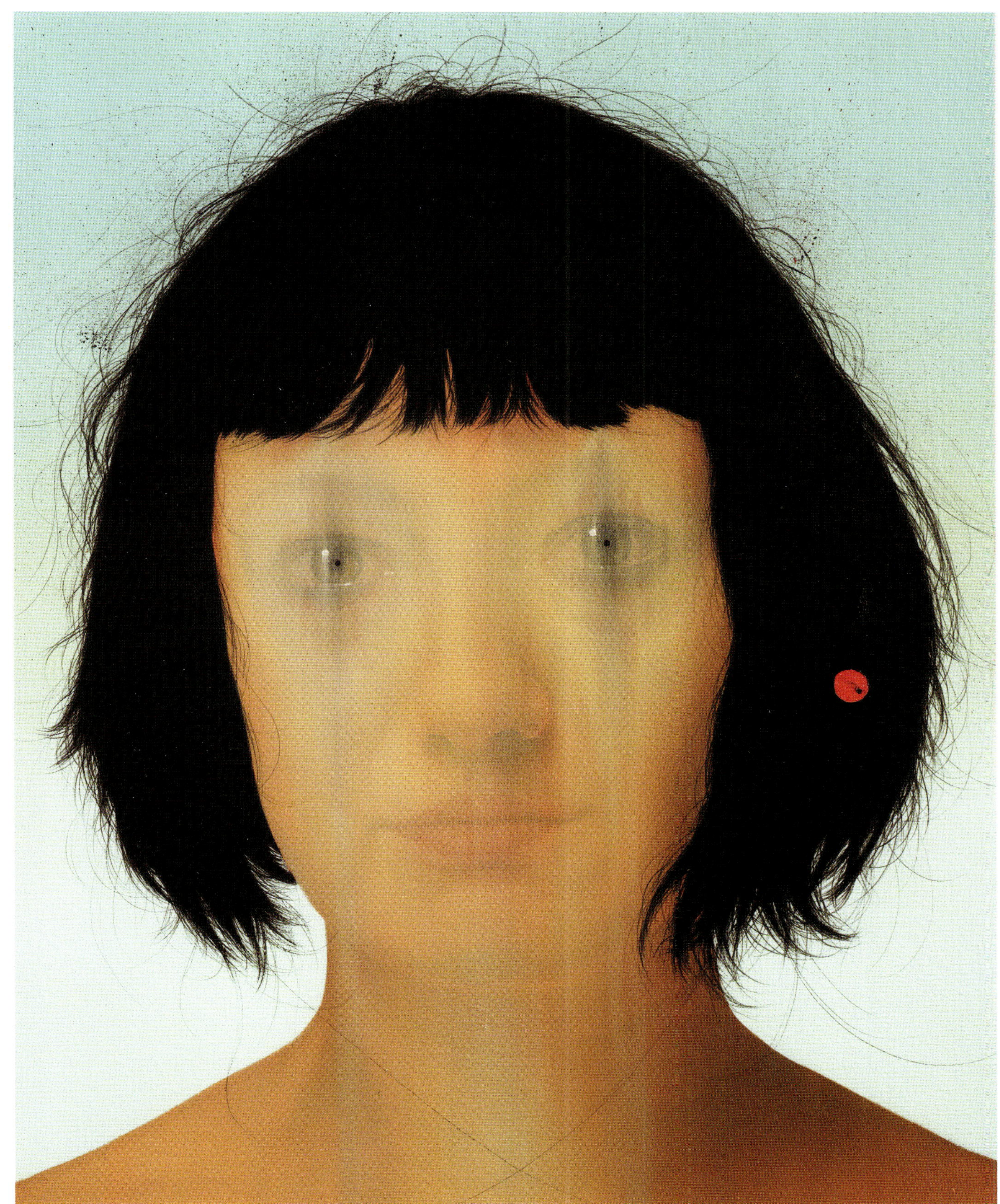

WE ARE NOT ALONE   2013   Oil on canvas   55 x 39 inches

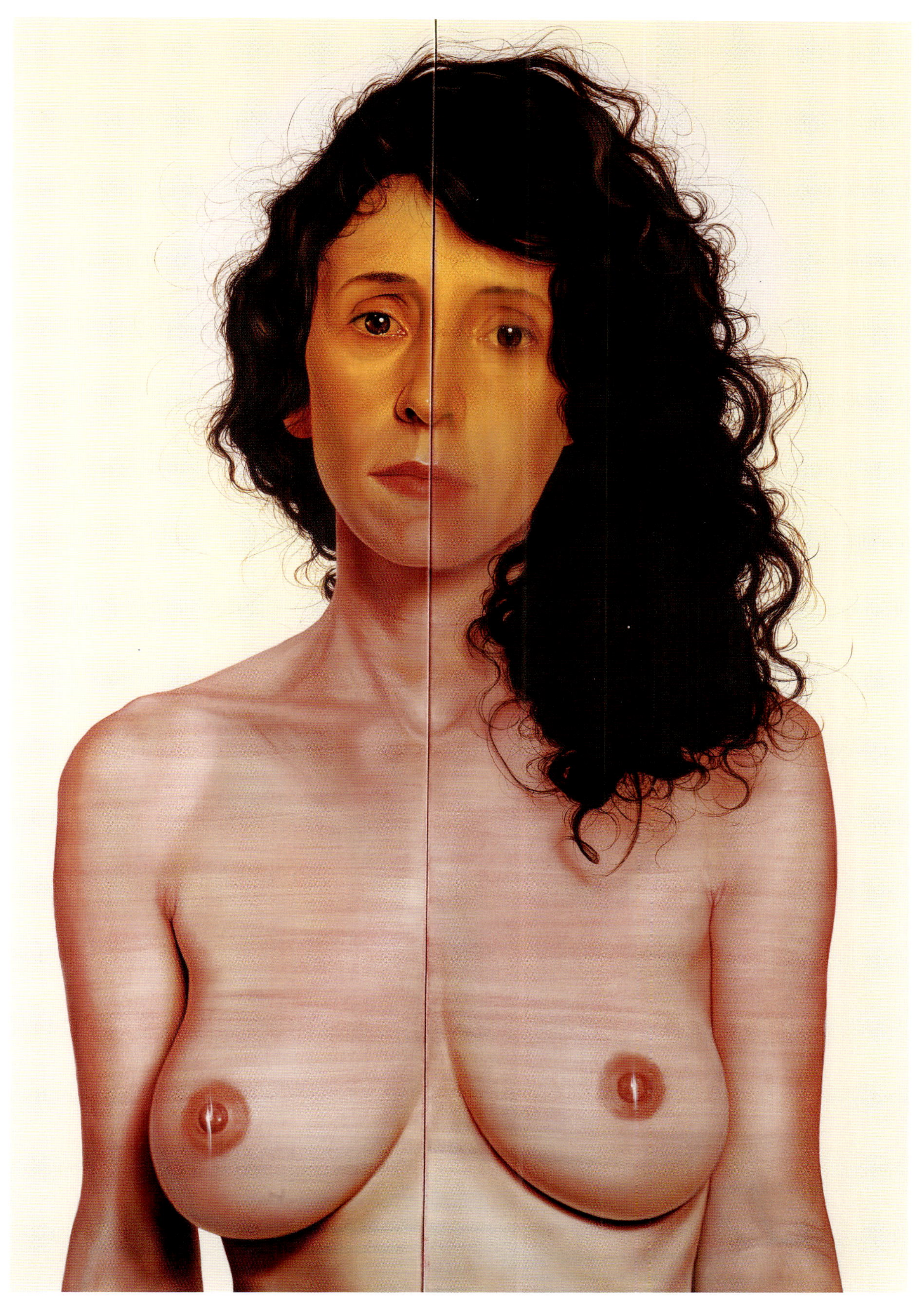

KINGS AND QUEENS   2013   Oil on canvas   84 x 150 inches

Detail on overleaf

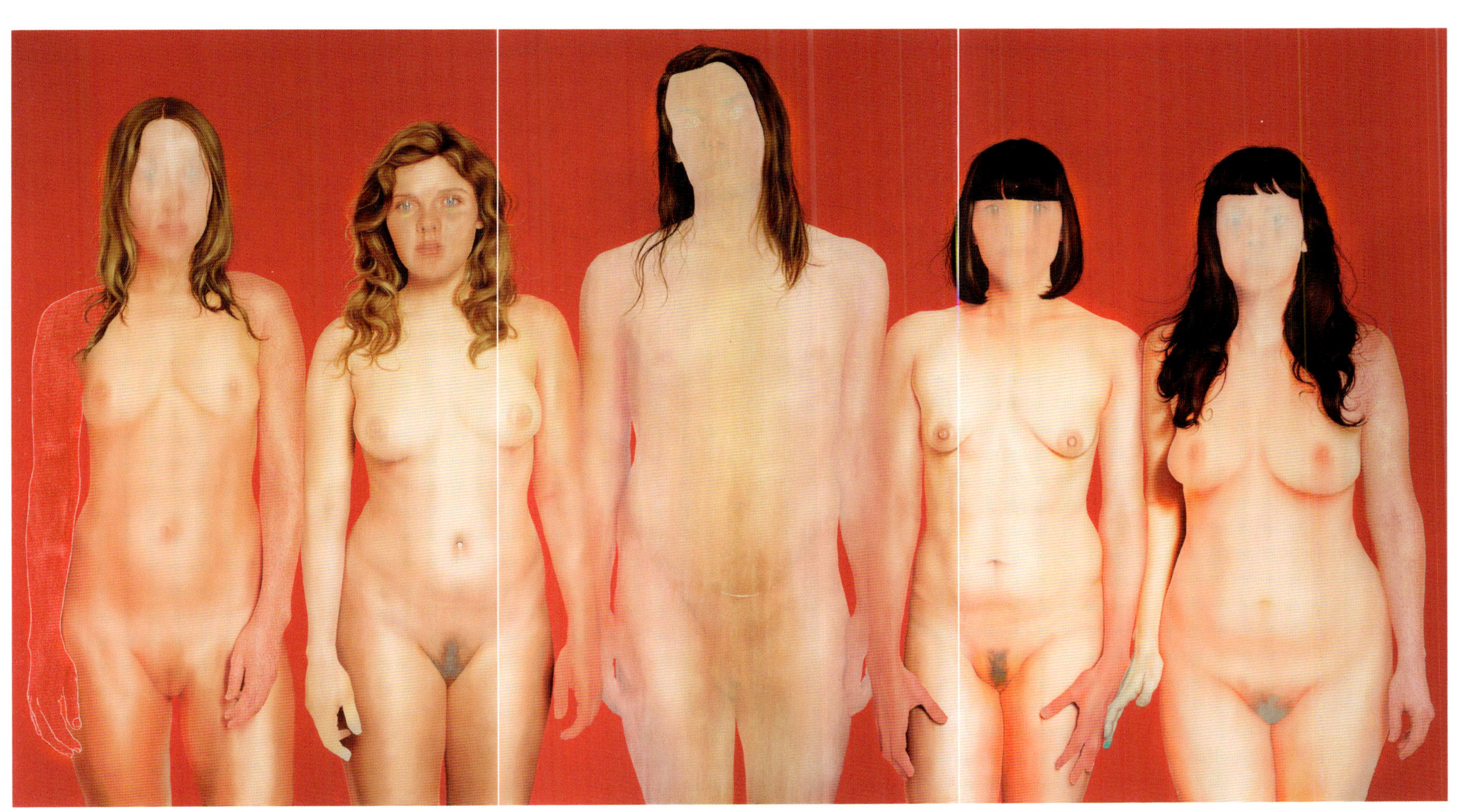

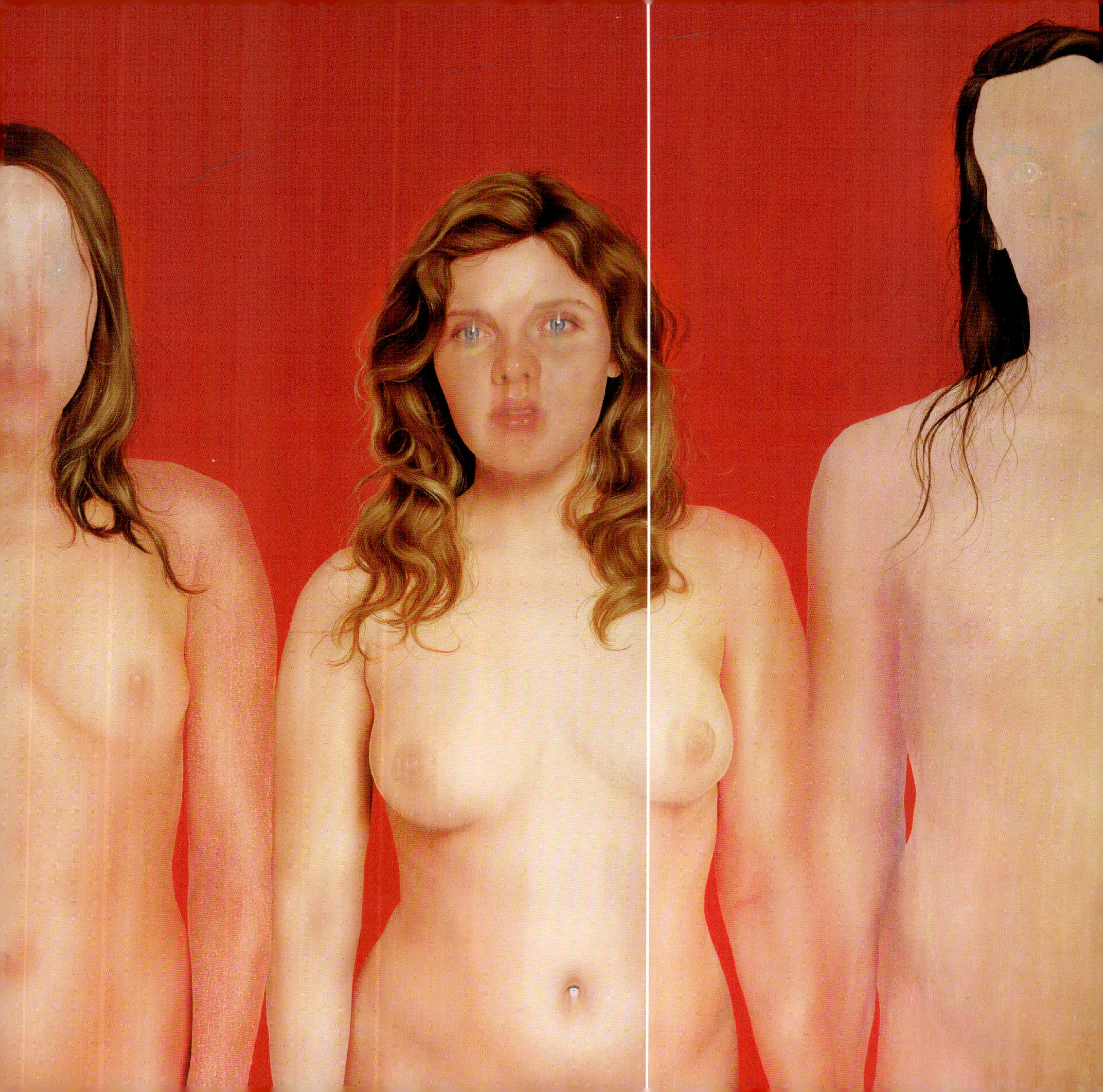

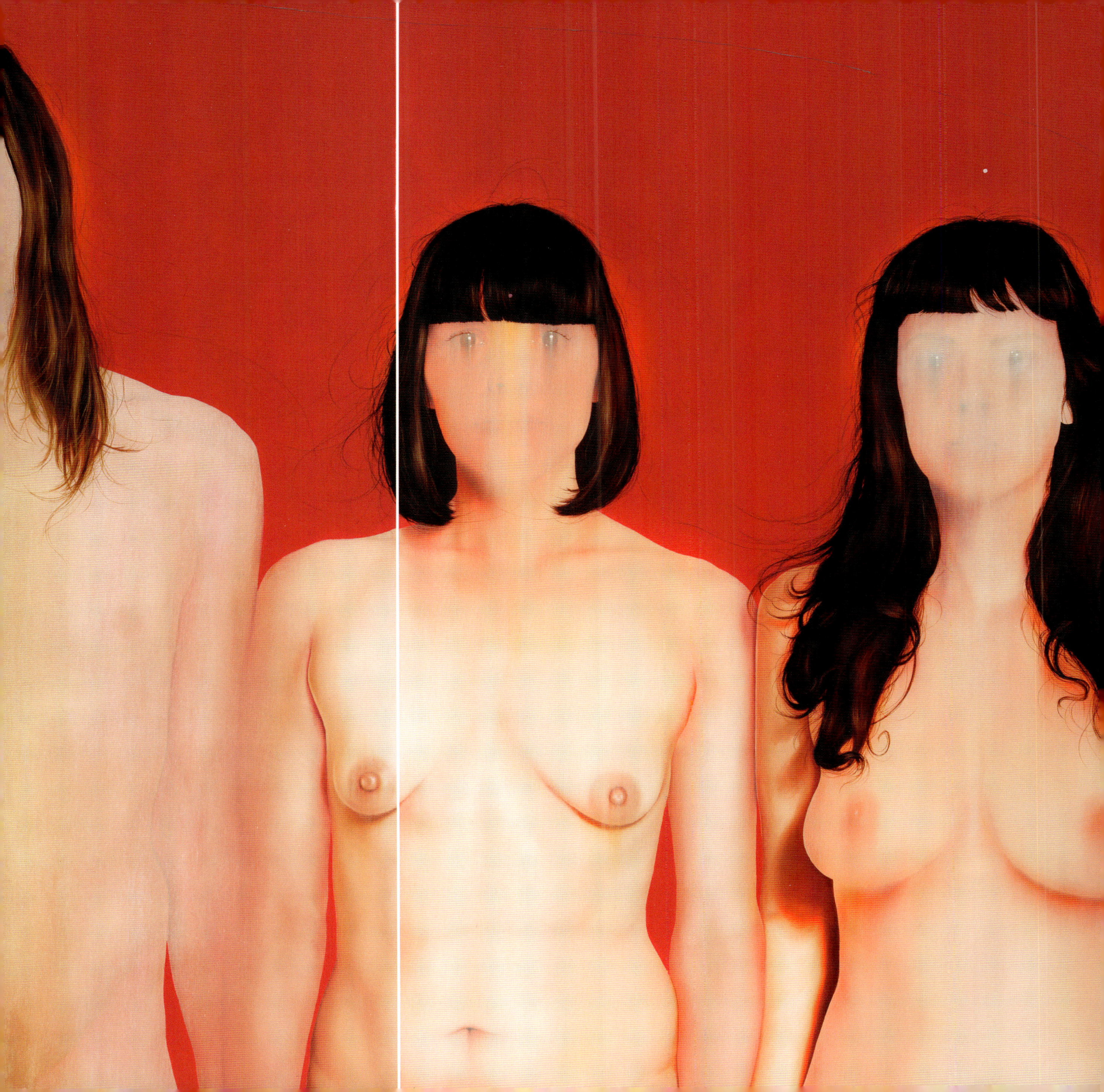

ME WHEN I'M WITH ANNE   2012   Oil on canvas   58 x 45 inches

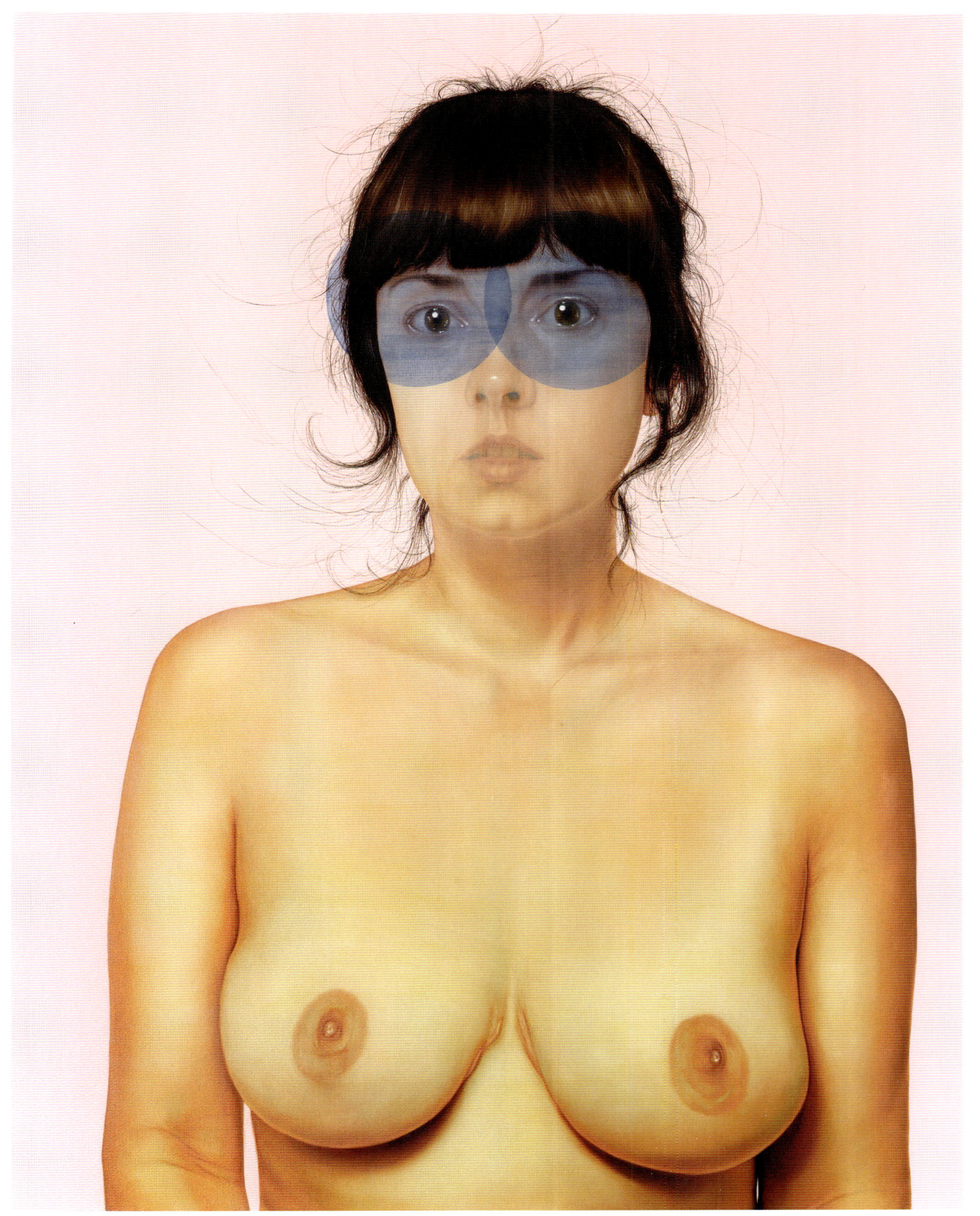

MENTOR   2012   Oil on canvas   77 x 52 inches

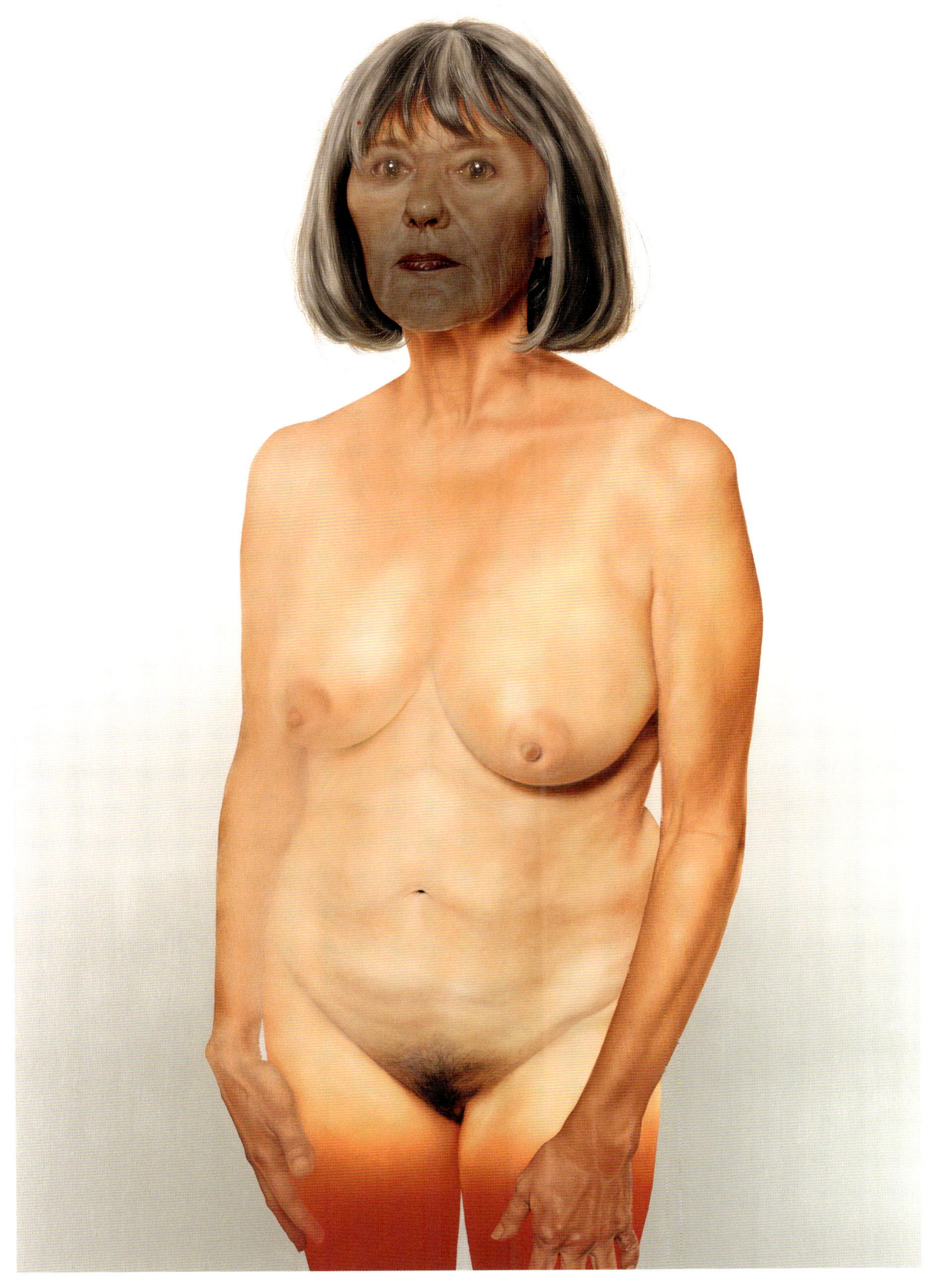

SHADOW   2012   Oil on canvas   40 x 32 ¼ inches
Private Collection, Colorado

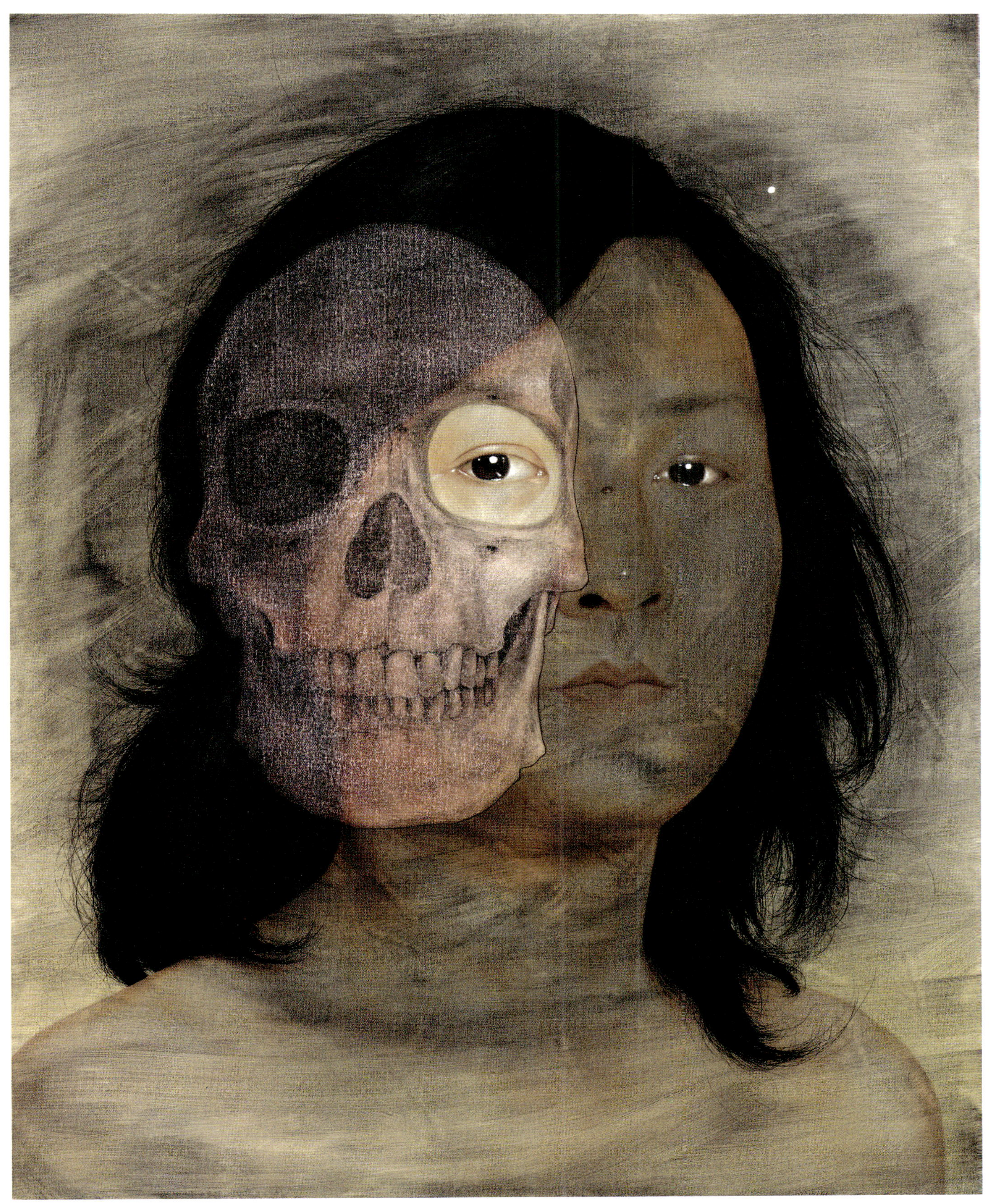

HIATUS   2012   Oil on canvas   78 x 52 inches

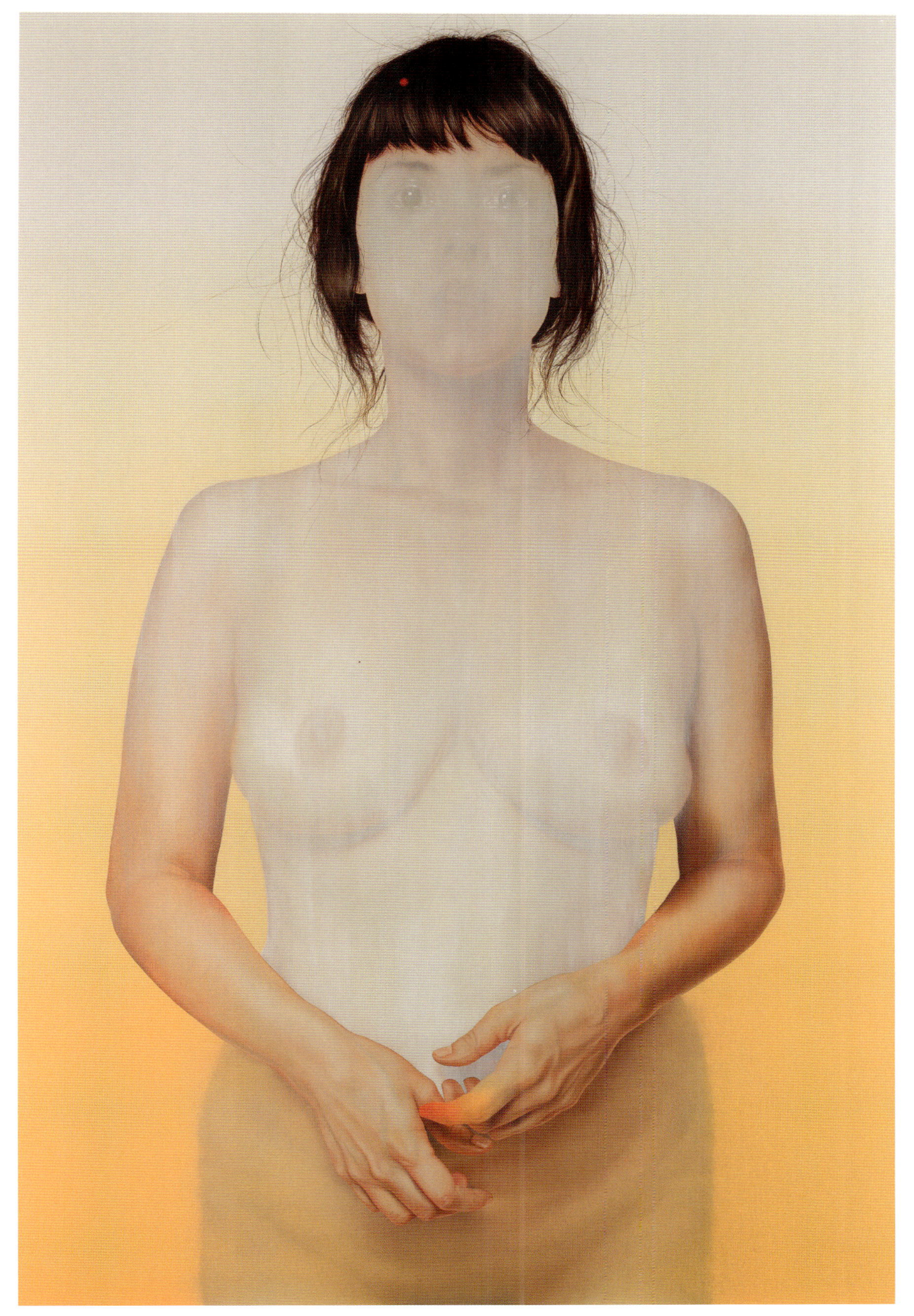

OH MY LOVE, WHAT A MIRROR REFLECTION WE ARE   2012   Oil on canvas   55 x 50 inches

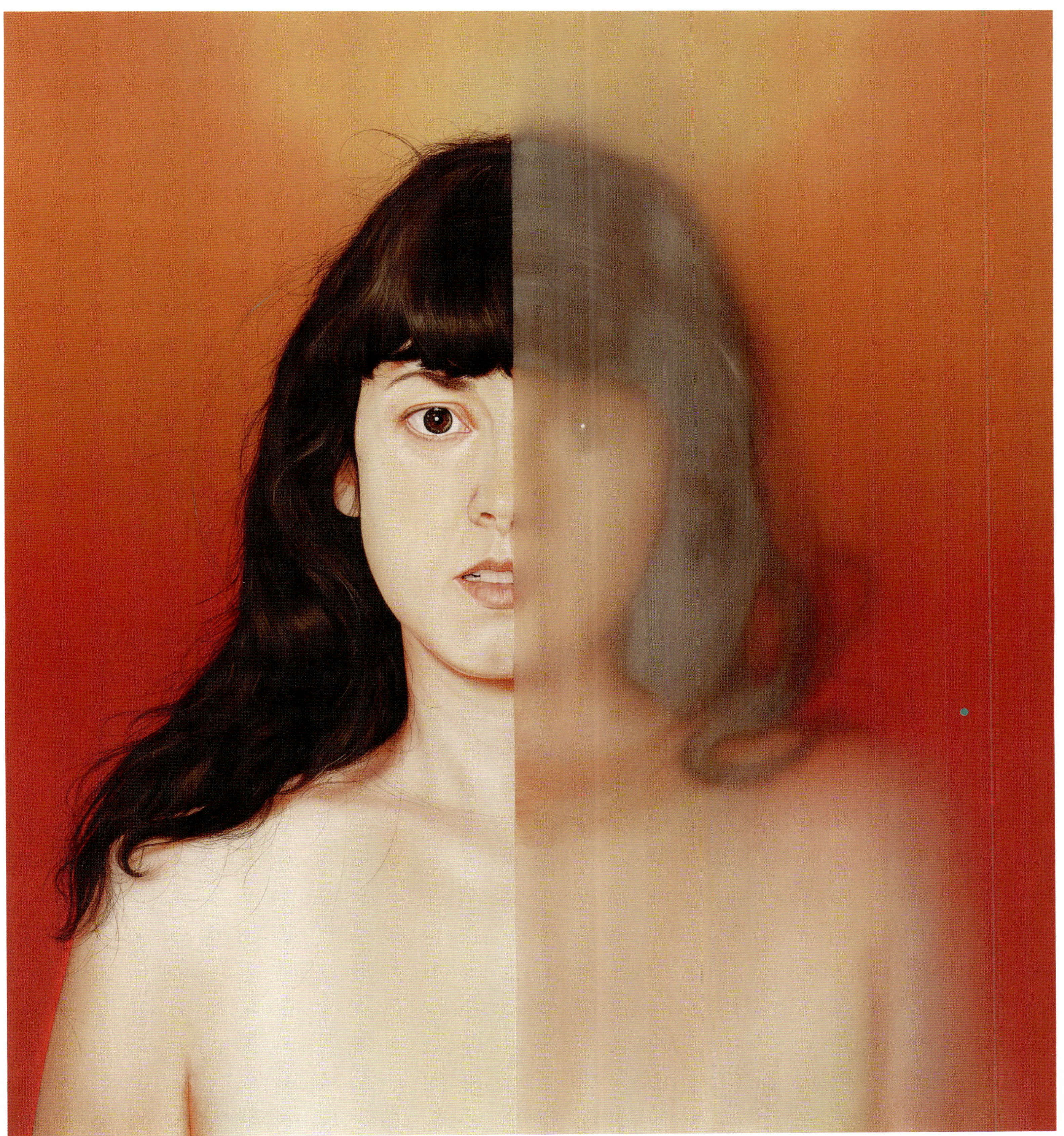

MERGING THE DOPPELGÄNGER   2012   Oil on canvas   40 x 34 inches
Private Collection, New York

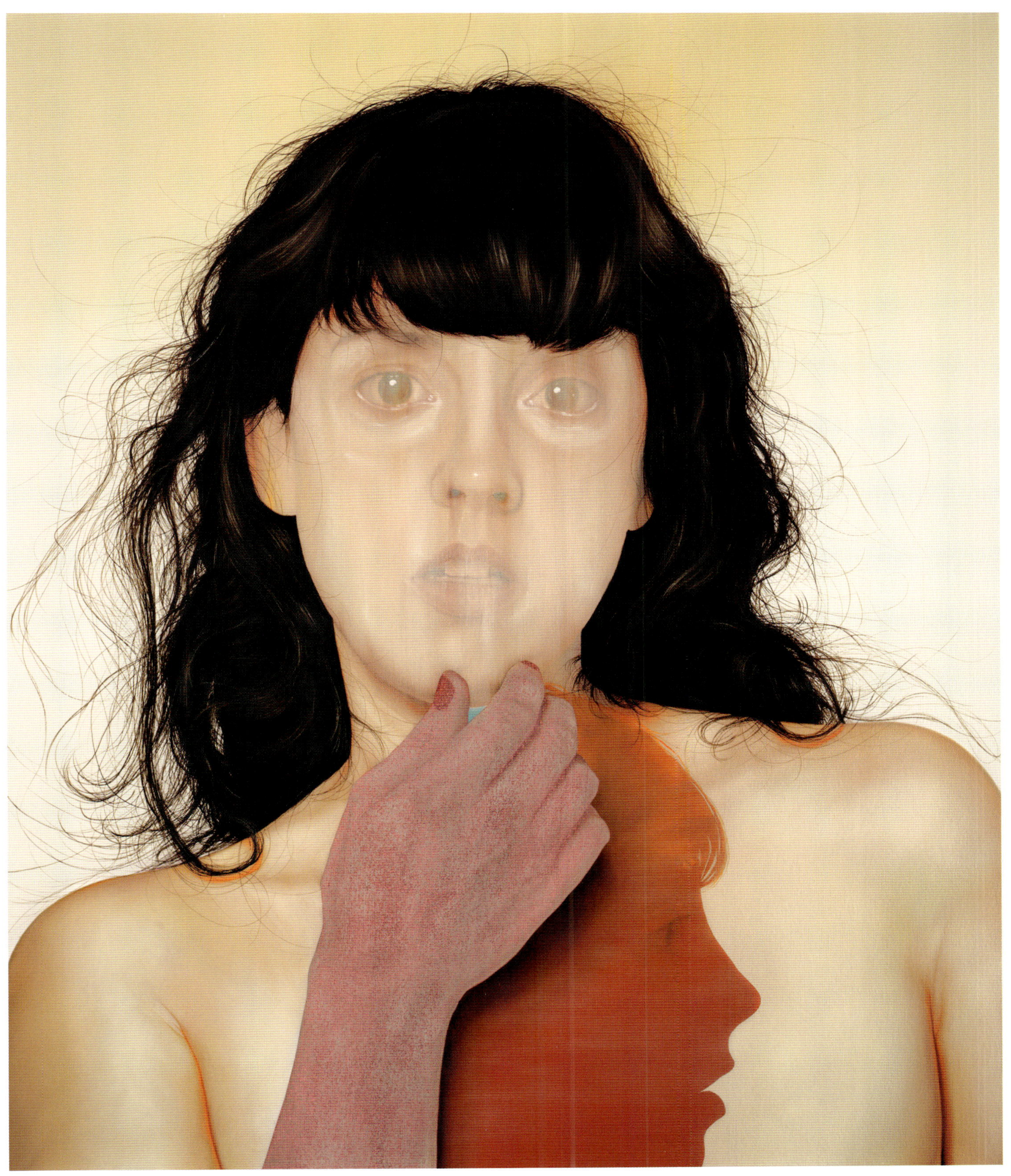

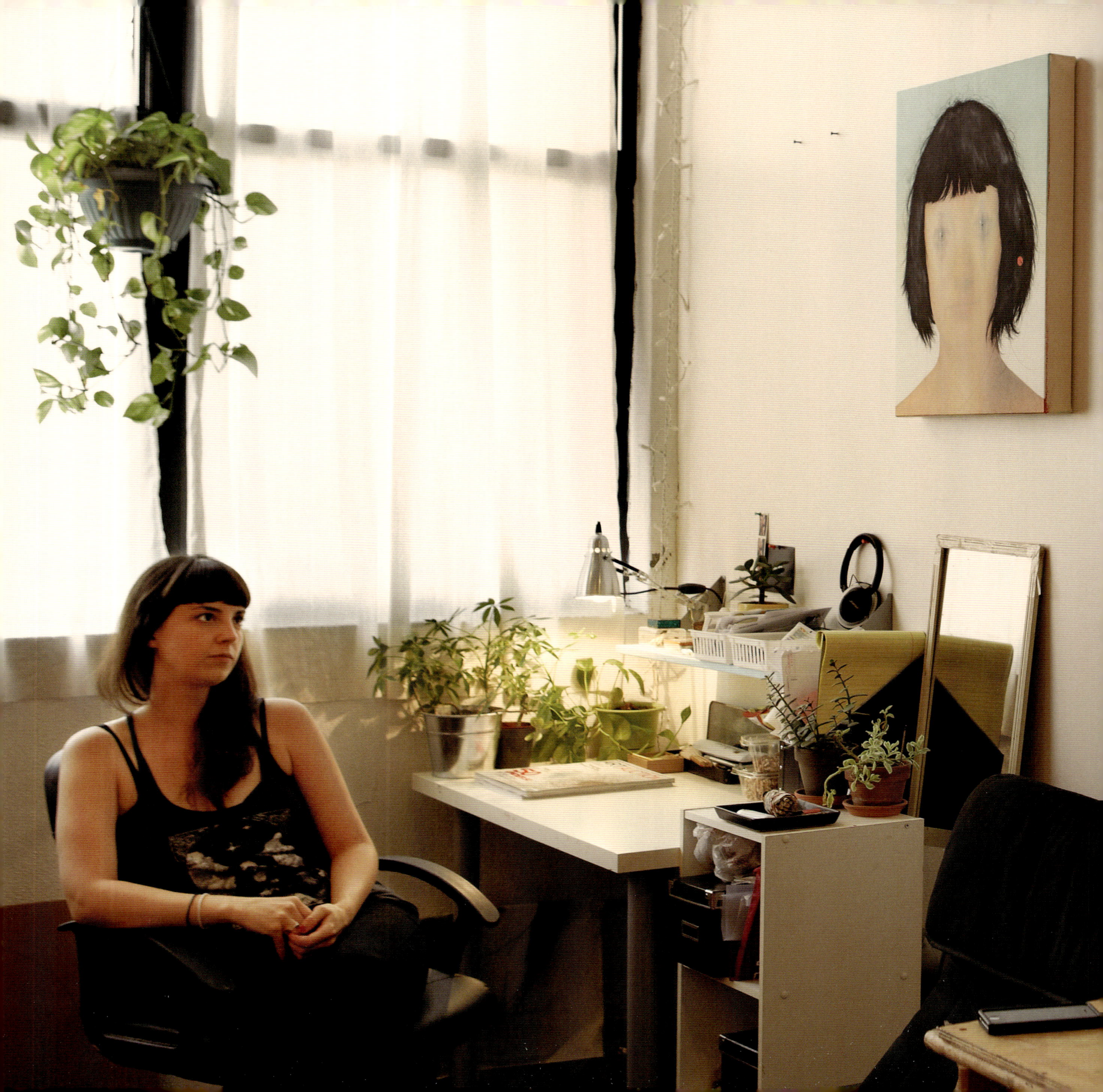

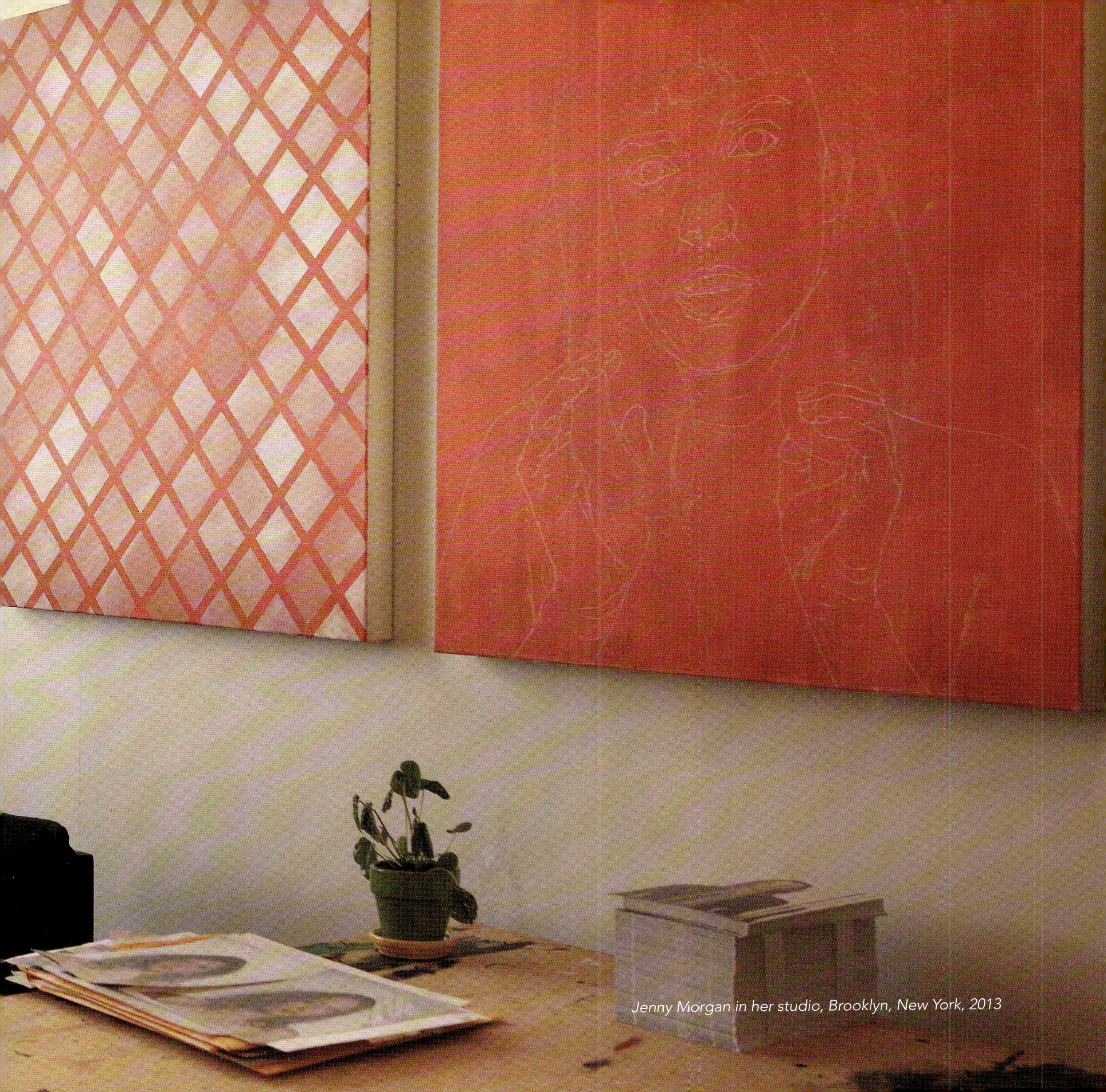

Jenny Morgan in her studio, Brooklyn, New York, 2013

SELECTED SOLO EXHIBITIONS

2013   Driscoll Babcock Galleries, New York, NY, *How To Find A Ghost*

2012   Plus Gallery, Denver, CO, *Kith and Kin*

2011   Like the Spice Gallery, Brooklyn, NY, *One and the Many*

2009   Plus Gallery, Denver, CO, *This Too Shall Pass*

        Like the Spice Gallery, Brooklyn, NY, *Abrasions*

2006   Plus Gallery, Denver, CO, *Romantic Comedies*

2005   Pirate Gallery, Denver, CO, *Mine Not Yours*

        Plus Gallery, Denver, CO, *First Person, Future Tense*

2004   Pirate Gallery, Denver, CO, *Soliloquies*

2003   Pirate Gallery, Denver, CO, *Delicate Disclosure*

        Phillip Steele Gallery, Denver, CO, *Jenny Morgan*

2002   Pirate Gallery, Denver, CO, *Spaces Between*

SELECTED GROUP EXHIBITIONS

2013   Salisbury University Art Galleries, MD, *Beyond Vision: Messages from the
        Holographic Universe*

        Nohra Haime Gallery, New York, NY, *Hard-Boiled Wonderland and the End of
        the World*

2012   Driscoll Babcock Galleries, New York, NY, *This Is How We Do It*

        Stephan Stoyanov Gallery, New York, NY, *Great Promise*

        Arvada Center for the Arts and Humanities, CO, *Faces*

        Victoria H. Myhren Gallery, University of Denver, CO, *Four x Four: Collector's Series*

        Center For Visual Art, Metropolitan State University of Denver, CO, *Out-Figured*

2011   Copro Gallery, Los Angeles, CA, *Dark Water*

        The Shirey Gallery, Brooklyn, NY, *Paint it Black*

        Pop Up Gallery, New York, NY, *Afterlife*

2010   The Magnificent Basement, London, UK, *Off the Clock*

        Tribeca 92Y, New York, NY, *Off the Clock*

SELECTED GROUP EXHIBITIONS, continued

Galleri Se Konst, Falun, Sweden, *Drawing Show*

Like the Spice Gallery, Brooklyn, NY, *Drift Away*

The Parlour, Brooklyn, NY, *See You in September*

Like the Spice Gallery, Brooklyn, NY, *Marked: A Show of Figure*

Visual Art Institute, Salt Lake City, UT, *Containment*

Plus Gallery, Denver, CO, *Excellencies*

Postmasters Gallery, New York, NY, *Mirror, Mirror*

2009   Postmasters Gallery, New York, NY, *Don't Flee the Art Market*

Like the Spice Gallery, Brooklyn, NY, *Civil Union*

Like the Spice Gallery, Brooklyn, NY, *Off the Clock*

2008   Millennia Gallery, Orlando, FL, *The Best and the Brightest*

The LeRoy Neiman Gallery, Columbia University, NY, *Face Forward*

Westside Gallery, New York, NY, *Open Secret*

Kravets/Wehby Gallery, New York, NY, *Pink Polemic,* curated by Erin Abraham

2007   Plus Gallery, Denver, CO, *Surprise!*

Mizel Arts and Culture Center, Denver, CO, *(New) Disasters of War*

Foothills Art Center, Golden, CO, *Relationships: Works of Surreal Inspiration*

2006-7 National Portrait Gallery, Smithsonian Institution, Washington, D.C., *The Outwin*

        Boochever Portrait Competition

2006   Plus Gallery, Denver, CO, *Romantic Comedies*

Museum of Contemporary Art; Center for Visual Arts; Gates Sculpture Triangle

        Park; Carol Keller Project Space, Denver, CO, *Decades of Influence:*

        Colorado 1985 – Present

2005   Pirate Gallery, Denver, CO, *Group Show*

LadyFest Out West, Denver, CO, with POD Gallery

Emmanuel Gallery, Denver, CO, *Figure Painting Invitational*

2004   HazMat Gallery, Denver, CO, *Open Reduction, Internal Fixation*

SELECTED BIBLIOGRAPHY

Alumni & Friends Newsletter. *Rocky Mountain College of Art and Design*, Summer 2006: Cover image.

"Best Bets." *Denver Post*. September 1, 2006.

Chandler, Mary Voelz. "Newly Hung Fall Exhibitions Exude Sense of Timelessness." Review of *Jenny Morgan: Romantic Comedies. Rocky Mountain News*. Web. 8 September. 2006.

------------. "Spotlight: Critic's Choice." *Rocky Mountain News*. Web. 10 August. 2003.

Commins, Ryan Michael. "Confronting the Moment." *Working Class Magazine*. April 2012: 9.

Cruz, Araceli. "About Face: Capturing Inner Beauty One Hair Strand at a Time." Review of *Jenny Morgan: One and the Many. Village Voice*. Web. 4 May. 2011.

Darnell, Meredith. "A Peak Into the Hearts and Minds of Colorado's Most Talented Artists." *Colorado Expressions Magazine*. August/September 2006: 80.

Goebel, Leanne Haase. "Painter Profile: Jenny Morgan." *Art Ltd. Magazine*. May/June 2010: Cover image, 48-49.

Haimerl, Amy. "Comedic Timing." Review of *Jenny Morgan: Romantic Comedies. Westword*. Web. 7 September. 2006.

MacMillan, Kyle. "'This Too Shall Pass' Artist Shows Staying Power." *Denver Post*. November 13, 2009.

Menendez, Didi. "Jenny Morgan." *Poets and Artists Magazine*. Fall 2010: 39-42.

Mills, Jack. "Jenny Morgan – Kith and Kin." Review. *Wonderland Magazine*. Web. 28 May. 2012.

Nedderman, Cheryl. "On the Rise: Jenny Morgan." *5280 Magazine*. July 2006: 28.

New American Paintings – Juried Exhibition-in-Print. Boston, MA: The Open Studios Press, 2005.

(New) Disasters of War: January 25-April 6, 2007. Denver, CO: Singer Gallery & Mizel Center
        for Arts and Culture, 2007.

Paglia, Michael. "Critic's Picks: Denver." Review of *Jenny Morgan: Kith and Kin. Art Ltd.
        Magazine*. Web. 28 July. 2012.

------------. "Extra Innings: Who's In – And Out – In My Fantasy Decades." Review of
        Decades of Influence: Colorado 1985 – Present. Westword. Web. 6 July. 2006.

------------. "Jenny Morgan's 'Psychological Portraits' Reveal Stunning Technical Skills."
        Review of *Jenny Morgan: Kith and Kin. Westword*. Web. 6 September. 2012.

------------. "They're Off: Impressive Solos at Havu and + Start the Season With a Bang."
        Westword. September 21-27, 2006: 52.

Schnabel, J.L. "Jenny Morgan." *Hi Fructose Magazine*, vol. 21. October 2011: 40-45.

Sutton, Benjamin. "Figuring it out in Williamsburg." Review of *Marked: A Show of Figure*.
        L Magazine. Web. 15 July. 2010.

------------. "Inside the Artist's Studio: Jenny Morgan in Bushwick." *L Magazine*. Web.
        11 May. 2011.

The Blind Architect. "Interview: Jenny Morgan." *Empty Kingdom*. Web. 29 June. 2012.

"Top of the Rocky: People." *Rocky Mountain News*. Web. 8 September. 2006.

Torke, Pamela. "10 Local Artists to Collect Now." *Colorado Homes and Lifestyles Magazine*.
        May 2006: 55.

Voynovskaya, Nastia. "New Work by Jenny Morgan." *Hi Fructose Magazine*. Web.
        24 July. 2012.

Zeile, Ivar. *Jenny Morgan: New Territory*. Denver, CO: Plus Gallery, 2009.

------------. *Jenny Morgan: We Are All Setting Suns*. Denver, CO: Plus Gallery, 2012.

Zimmer, Lori. "Six of One: Six Quick Questions With One of My Favorite Artists." *PMc
        Magazine*. Web. August 2011.

LIST OF ILLUSTRATIONS

BIOGRAPHY

Corporeal but also ethereal, Jenny Morgan pushes the boundaries of figurative painting by exploring new ways of affecting her impeccably detailed images. Her haunting portraits are perfectly realized only to be annihilated; their surfaces sanded and stripped away to reveal physical and spiritual wounds of the flesh. By disturbing the surface of the canvas, she achieves a striking intensity and psychological depth in her work, breaking through the ideals of traditional portraiture and the preciousness of realism. Morgan's deeply personal work examines the complexity of human relationships and awareness, providing the viewer a visual and conceptual window into the vulnerable multiplicities of the self.

Since 2012, Jenny Morgan has been exclusively represented by Driscoll Babcock Galleries. Morgan's work has been exhibited nationwide and internationally in solo exhibitions at galleries in Brooklyn, New York and Denver, Colorado; and in numerous group exhibitions including the Smithsonian National Portrait Gallery, in Washington, D.C.; 92Y Tribeca and the Le Roy Neiman Gallery at Columbia University, both in New York; and at galleries in Orlando, Florida; London, England; and Falun, Sweden. Additionally, Morgan has realized several portraiture commissions for the likes of *The New York Times Magazine* and *New York Magazine*.

Her work is represented in major private collections throughout the United States.

Born in Salt Lake City, Utah, Jenny Morgan currently lives and works in Brooklyn, New York. She holds a BA from the Rocky Mountain College School of Design in Lakewood, Colorado and an MFA from the School of Visual Arts in New York.

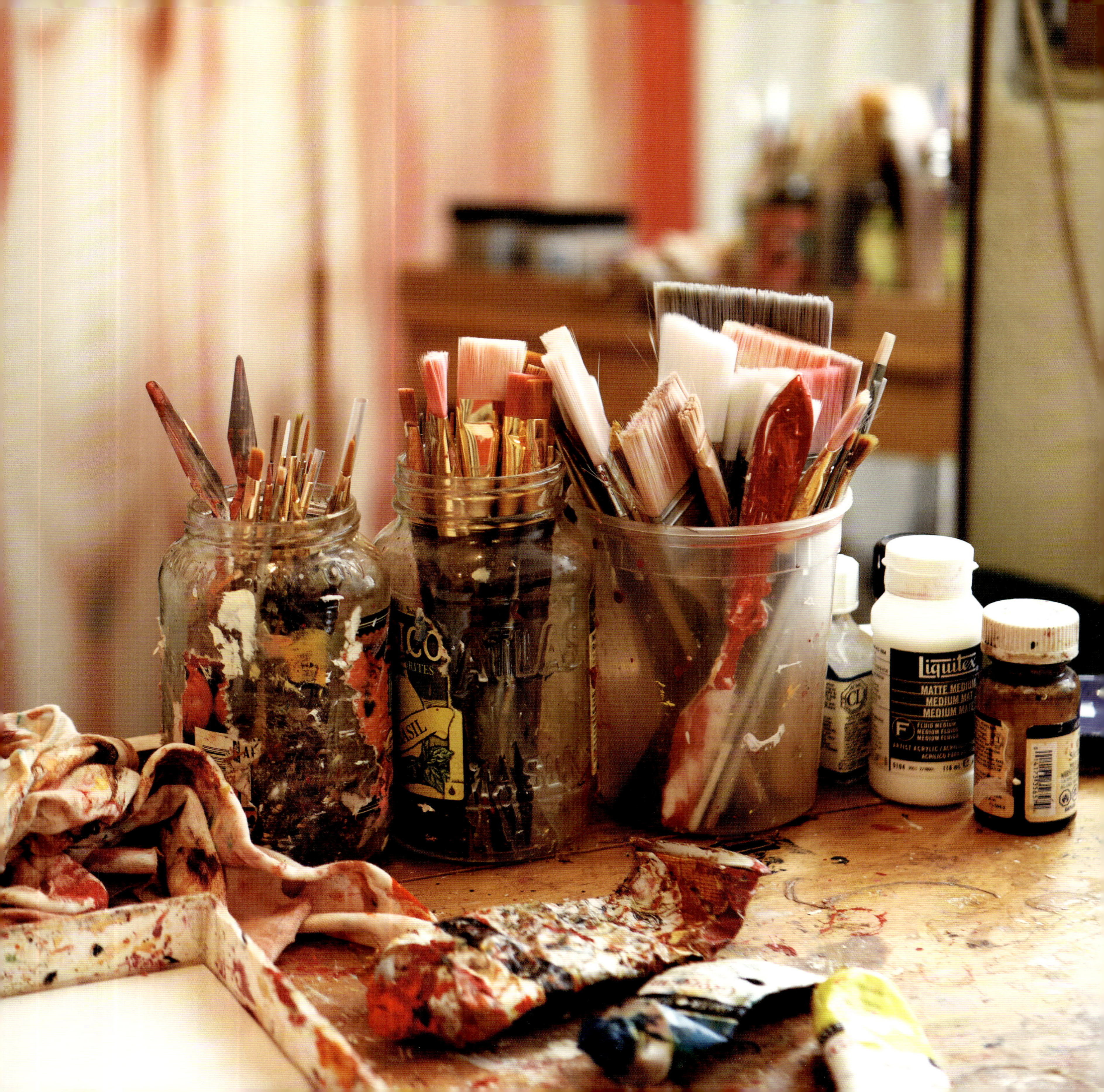

ACKNOWLEDGEMENTS

First and foremost, I would like to acknowledge my parents Lynn and Ruth Morgan. Without their unconditional support throughout my life, none of this would be possible. From an early age, I was encouraged to express my creativity and was taught that making and creating was more than just an enjoyable activity, but also a valuable skill. I was shown through example that being an artist could lead to a rewarding life and professional career. I am profoundly grateful for their continual love and belief in me.

Next would be my beloved muses. I would like to thank David Mramor, Syrie Moskowitz, Stacy Scibelli, Agata Bebecka, Natalia Yovane, Rocio Salceda, Cara Despain, Adriane Schramm, Noa and Maya Charuvi-Shai and last but not least, Wolfie the cat. I feel blessed to be surrounded by these individuals who are extraordinary artists and musicians in their own right. Trust is the most important element in the artist/model relationship, and I am honored that these beautiful people have allowed me to see them at their most vulnerable—I cherish this gift.

I would like to acknowledge Ivar Zeile who took a chance on a young artist fresh out of college and gave me the first solo show of my career at Plus Gallery in Denver, Colorado. Ivar has been a stable force propelling my career and work forward for the last decade. His endless faith in me has supplied strength during the trying times, and his tireless efforts supported my livelihood through graduate school and beyond. Plus Gallery has become an extended family, and I feel fortunate to know such caring, hardworking souls.

I want acknowledge Marisa Sage for her powerful dedication during my four years with Like the Spice Gallery in Brooklyn, New York, which proved to be a pivotal point in my development. Marisa gave me my first solo show and representation in New York City. She provided a platform for growth and experimentation within this intense city and introduced me to a broad audience. Marisa's efforts allowed John Driscoll to view and purchase my work which lead to my representation with Driscoll Babcock Galleries.

I want to thank John Driscoll for inviting me into Driscoll Babcock Galleries. This relationship is a dream come true for me, and I am immensely grateful for this opportunity. John and his Director, Tess Sol Schwab, entered my studio with a full breadth of art historical knowledge and are able to peer deeply into the heart of my work. The staff as whole is a reflection of John's genuine love for what he does, and I feel honored to be working with such sincere

Left: Jenny Morgan's studio, Brooklyn, New York, 2013

and devoted people.

My collectors have been a constant support and essential part of my practice. Through conversation about the work with these dedicated individuals, I have gained a deeper understanding of my own process and content. I would like to specifically thank Dr. Wayne Yakes for his passionate investment in my career and his thoughtful insights into the work. Thank you to Bob and Pam Neufeld who have incorporated my work into their lives with loving generosity since 2004. I also want to thank Brian Tschumper, Ali Theriault and Ron Guillot, Jennifer and Dave Korman, Dave and Candace Johnson, Norman Dubrow, Glen and Margret Wood, Graham and Jaqueline Mills, Lorie Bilker and Gregory Kong, Jeffery Manocherian and Howard Tullman.

I get by with a little help from my friends. I want acknowledge the friends who have had faith in me from the very beginning. Thank you to Caitlin Rapp and family for being a home away from home and willing subject matter for over 20 years. Thank you to Anya Zeitlin for her innate confidence in me—she generously acted as my assistant, pro bono, for two years, which was such a gift. Kenny Riches has been an artistic soul mate since adolescence and continues to inspire me. I wouldn't have survived New York without my fellow School of Visual Arts alumni—thank you to David Mramor, Gregg Louis, Stacy Scibelli, Amber Broadmam, Natalia Yovane, Katie Cummings, Trish Tillman, Brandon Davey and Stan Narten for the late night crits, which always buoy my spirit. And I want to acknowledge Tim Pourbaix whose love is unparalleled—I feel blessed to have him in my life.

I want to thank the magical Marilyn Minter and her studio for giving me one of the best jobs in the world. Marilyn's passionate dedication was a shining example of what it takes to be a true artist. The lessons I learned about painting and running a studio are invaluable. I will never forget the hilarious lunchtime conversations, the birthday party bus and the ever-transforming gnome.

And finally, I want to acknowledge all who have supported me through the years by attending openings, writing letters and being present for lectures. I am immensely grateful to be a part of the art world and share my personal voice with the greater whole. Thank you.

Jenny Morgan, 2013